The Peaceful Palate

Fine Vegetarian Cuisine

by Jennifer Raymond

Heart & Soul Publications
1418 Cedar Street
Calistoga, California 94515

For information contact: Heart and Soul Publications
                             1418 Cedar Street
                             Calistoga, California 94515-1610

Revised Edition

Cover illustration and illustrations on pages 8, 9, & 10 by Andy Miller.

Cover design by Cheryl Karas.

Library of Congress Cataloging-in-Publication Data

Raymond, Jennifer
    The peaceful palate : vegetarian's favorite cookbook : bountiful,
beautiful, easy, low-fat & delilcious / Jennifer Raymond.
      p. cm.
    Includes index.
    ISBN 1-57067-031-6
    1. Vegetarian cookery. 2. Low-fat diet--Recipes. 3. Quick and easy
cookery.   I. Title.
    TX837.R38 1996
    641.5'636--dc20
                                    96-3806
                                      CIP

Dedicated to all seekers of peace

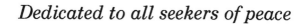

*Until he extends the circle of his compassion to all living things,
man will not himself find peace.*

Albert Schweitzer

Peace On Earth

Isn't man an amazing Animal? He kills wildlife—birds, kangaroos, deer, all kinds of cats, coyotes, beavers, groundhogs, mice, foxes, and dingoes—by the million in order to protect his domestic animals and their feed.

Then he kills domestic animals by the billion and eats them. This in turn kills man by the million, because eating all those animals leads to degenerative—and fatal—health conditions like heart disease, kidney disease, and cancer.

So then man tortures and kills millions more animals to look for cures for these diseases.

Elsewhere, millions of other human beings are being killed by hunger and malnutrition because food they could eat is being used to fatten domestic animals.

Meanwhile, some people are dying of sad laughter at the absurdity of man, who kills so easily and so violently, and once a year sends out cards praying for "Peace on Earth."

from *Old MacDonald's Factory Farm* by C. David Coats

Contents

Acknowledgements

My deepest thanks to all of the people who contributed in so many ways to this book: friends, students, and family.

In particular, I'd like to thank Patti Breitman for her unflagging enthusiasm, vision, and encouragement.

Thanks to Adrien Avis, my wonderful mother-by-marriage, for her love, her tireless proofreading, and her many excellent suggestions.

Many thanks to Andy Miller for the cover art and his drawings of animals. Thanks to Sheryl Karas for her excellent cover design, and to Denise Mannor of BookCrafters, who patiently guided me through the maze of publication details.

Thanks to my faithful canine companions, Jasper, Millie, MacKenzie, Merlin, and Grady Tucker, who waited patiently as I tested recipes and typed.

Finally, special thanks to Stephen Avis, my husband and companion-in-life, who is always there for me. Without him, this book would not have been possible.

Introduction

Vegetarian cuisine has turned several corners since the publication of my first book, *The Best of Jenny's Kitchen*. It has become at once simpler and more sophisticated. The notion of protein complementarity, the idea that certain foods need to be eaten together to provide complete protein, has been replaced by the knowledge that plenty of high quality protein is obtained simply by eating a variety of wholesome foods throughout the day. In other words, you don't need to struggle with complicated protein-combining charts.

Health experts now recognize that most Americans actually eat too much protein, with several negative consequences including kidney disease and osteoporosis. Our daily protein requirement is quite modest and easily met by the grains, beans, and fresh vegetables included in a vegetarian diet. As a result, vegetarian cooking has become lighter and fresher, less reliant on heavy egg and cheese dishes.

While the protein contributed by animal foods is excessive, the fat is downright lethal. Heart disease, cancer, obesity, and adult-onset diabetes are but a few of the consequences of a high fat diet. The average American consumes nearly half of his or her calories each day from fat, primarily from meat, dairy products, and eggs. In light of recommendations by health experts to significantly reduce dietary fat, the new vegetarian cuisine focuses on plant foods—grains, beans, vegetables, and fruits. These foods are low in fat, and the fat they do contain is mostly of the healthier unsaturated variety.

Even as fat has become a villain in the dietary drama, complex carbohydrate has emerged the hero. Once maligned as fattening, complex carbohydrate (also known as "starch") is the body's perfect energy food, and should constitute the majority of each day's calories. Foods which are high in complex carbohydrate also provide fiber, which helps lower blood cholesterol and maintains a healthy digestive tract. Whole grains, beans and peas, potatoes, fresh vegetables and fruits are all excellent sources of complex carbohydrate, and serve as the mainstay of a healthful diet.

The recipes which follow reflect these nutritional principles. They also reflect the belief that to cause unnecessary suffering and death of any creature is wrong. Animals live and die terribly, so that humans might eat foods which are not only unnecessary, but actually detrimental to health. By improving our own diets and lives, we can spare the cows and calves, the sheep and lambs, the pigs and chickens and turkeys. Our food can become a true celebration of life, for all beings.

I hope you will enjoy these recipes, this celebration of all life.

Jennifer Raymond
Calistoga, California

Choosing Food for Optimum Health

Food is composed of carbohydrate, protein, fat, vitamins, minerals, and water. For ideal health, these nutrients should be consumed in certain proportions each day.

Carbohydrate, or more specifically, *complex carbohydrate*, is the body's ideal energy source. Contrary to popular belief, complex carbohydrate, also known as *starch*, is not fattening. As a matter of fact, a diet high in complex carbohydrate is the best way to avoid gaining excess weight. Starch is the nutrient we should be consuming in the greatest quantity: 70 to 80 percent of each day's calories. Since complex carbohydrate is found only in plant foods—grains, beans, nuts, vegetables, and fruits—it is obvious that these foods should be the basis for all our meals.

Protein is used by the body for growth, maintenance, and repair. The body's need for protein is surprisingly small—only 10 percent of daily calories—and amounts in excess of this may cause kidney disease and osteoporosis. Animal foods greatly exceed the human protein requirement. Plant foods, which contain more moderate amounts of protein are much better suited to the human body's needs.

Fat is a concentrated source of energy and has more than twice the calories of either carbohydrate or protein. Fat should supply no more than 20 percent of each day's calories. Americans consume about twice this amount as a result of eating animal products which are high in fat, especially saturated fat. Unrefined plant foods, with the exception of seeds, nuts, olives, and avocados, are very low in fat.

The following table compares the calorie composition of an ideal diet with the calorie composition of animal and plant foods:

Ideal Diet	% Carbohydrate	% Protein	% Fat
	70-80	10	10-20
Animal Foods	% Carbohydrate	% Protein	% Fat
Red Meat	0	30	70
Fish	0	50-90	10-50
Poultry	0	50-70	30-50
Cheese	0	30	70
Eggs	0	30	70
Plant Foods			
Grains	80	10	10
Beans	70	25	5
Vegetables	70	25	5
Nuts	10	10	80
Fruits	90	5	5

The table makes it clear that animal products contain no complex carbohydrate and too much protein and fat. By contrast, plant foods (except for nuts) are primarily complex carbohydrate. They contain adequate, but not excessive, protein and fat. It is obvious that the diet for optimum health is one that is based on plant foods. Plant foods should be the center of each and every meal, and on pages 16 and 17 you will find menu suggestions for a variety of delicious and satisfying plant-based meals.

Protein

I suspect that if people on the street were asked the question "What is the most important nutrient?" the response would be almost unanimous: "PROTEIN!" And if asked where we get our protein, the answer again would probably be unanimous: "meat, eggs, and dairy products." To put it mildly, Americans have a protein obsession, and this not an accident. The meat and dairy industries spend billions of dollars each year promoting their protein-rich products in the media and in our schools.

While protein is indeed necessary for the body's growth, repair and maintenance, we actually need rather small amounts to meet these requirements. Women need about 44 grams per day (less than two ounces); the requirement for men is 56 grams (about two ounces). To put this in perspective, the average meat-eating American consumes between 100 and 150 grams of protein each day! A lacto-ovo vegetarian eats about 90 grams of protein each day, and the average vegan ("vee-gan"), who eats no animal products, consumes about 76 grams of protein. In other words, even individuals who consume no animal products more than meet their protein requirements.

It should be apparent from the above information that protein is not unique to meat, dairy products and eggs: it is found in all whole (non-junk) foods. We find protein in broccoli, wheat, lentils, and oatmeal. Corn and carrots, potatoes and pasta all contain protein. Simply eating a variety of these foods and others like them each day will supply plenty of protein.

Furthermore, protein complementarity, the idea of combining certain foods within each meal to get complete protein (or "complementary" amino acids), has been shown to be unnecessary. It is now known that amino acids from one food have several hours within which to be paired with complementary amino acids from other foods. Thus, by eating a variety of foods throughout the day, plenty of quality protein is obtained.

Health experts now recognize that most Americans eat too much protein, resulting in negative consequences including kidney disease and osteoporosis. When more protein than necessary is consumed the excess is burned for energy or is converted to fat. In the course of this process, nitrogen, sulfur compounds and other by-products are removed by the liver and excreted by the kidneys. As a result both the liver and kidneys are overworked when excess protein is consumed.

Furthermore, consumption of excess protein, particularly animal protein, causes calcium to be removed from the bones and excreted in the urine. We cannot compensate for this calcium loss by eating calcium-rich foods or taking supplements, because our bodies simply will not absorb calcium fast enough to replace the losses. As a result, a person on a high protein diet is constantly losing more calcium from the bones than is being replaced, eventually leading to weakening of the bones and osteoporosis. The way to prevent this problem is to decrease protein intake, and the easiest way to do this is to eliminate meat, dairy products, and eggs. The foods which are left—grains, beans, nuts, vegetables, and fruits—provide plenty of protein to meet all of the body's requirements, and they do it without overloading the body with protein like animal foods do. It should be noted that vegetable proteins do not cause as much calcium to be lost in the urine as do animal proteins. Thus, even though vegetarians and vegans may exceed the protein requirement, their risk of osteoporosis is less than that of meat eaters.

Calcium

As mentioned in the preceding section, decreasing the amount of protein you eat is one of the most important things you can do to protect your body's calcium. Getting adequate calcium is also important, and at this point you may be asking how to get sufficient calcium without consuming dairy products. The American Dairy Council has done an admirable job convincing us of the necessity of dairy products as calcium sources. Unfortunately, they are not telling the whole story.

In countries such as the People's Republic of China, where little or no milk is consumed, osteoporosis is rare. The Chinese get all their calcium (400 to 500 milligrams per day) from dark leafy green vegetables and other plant foods. Their bones remain strong throughout their lives. By contrast, in the United States, where large quantities of dairy products are consumed and calcium intake is between 800 and 1000 milligrams per day, osteoporosis is rampant. In other words, dairy products have not been effective in preventing osteoporosis.

In addition to calcium, dairy products contain appreciable amounts of protein and fat. Excess dietary protein, as discussed in the preceding section, causes calcium to be lost from the body, and fat may interfere with the absorption of calcium in the intestine.

Dark leafy green vegetables, such as collard greens, kale, and broccoli are excellent sources of calcium, and studies have shown that the calcium in these vegetables is better absorbed and utilized by the body than the calcium in milk. Soyfoods (especially tofu made with calcium), nuts and seeds, dried beans, sea vegetables, oranges, dried figs, and corn tortillas are also good sources of calcium. The fact is that many foods contain calcium, and by eating a varied diet you will get plenty of calcium to meet your needs.

How much calcium do you actually need? The United States requirement for adults is 800 to 1200 milligrams per day, while the World Health Organization recommends just 500 milligrams per day. The United States requirement is purposely inflated in an attempt to compensate for the large calcium losses caused by a high protein intake. Individuals who consume less protein, such as vegetarians and vegans, require less calcium, and the World Health Organization requirement seems an appropriate guideline. This is supported by several studies showing that vegetarians in the United States have significantly lower rates of osteoporosis than meat-eaters.

Protein Myths and Facts

Myth: *We need to eat a lot of protein to be healthy.*
Fact: While it is true that protein is essential, the amount we need each day is quite small: about 50 grams, or 10 percent of each day's calories, is plenty for adults.

Myth: *It's hard to get enough protein.*
Fact: Protein is found in almost all foods. Americans eat two to three times more protein than they actually need each day.

Myth: *Protein is only found in animal foods.*
Fact: Protein is found in plant foods as well as in animal foods. Grains, beans, nuts, seeds, and vegetables all provide protein. Eating a variety of these foods each day supplies plenty of protein, without the saturated fat and cholesterol of animal protein sources.

Myth: *Plant protein is inferior to animal protein.*
Fact: Plant protein is made up of the same building blocks, called "amino acids," as animal protein. Your body uses these amino acids to make the protein it needs. As far as your body is concerned, it makes no difference whether these amino acids come from plant or animal sources.

Myth: *Eating a lot of high-protein foods provides the body with a margin of safety.*
Fact: Eating excess protein provides no margin of safety, because the body cannot store protein. When you eat more protein than you need, your body simply converts it to fat or burns it for energy.

Myth: *Eating excess protein can't hurt you.*
Fact: Consumption of excess protein overworks the liver and kidneys, and may lead to disease of these organs. Consumption of excess protein causes the bones to lose calcium, leading to osteoporosis. One of the most effective ways to prevent osteoporosis is to moderate your protein intake.

Myth: *Getting enough protein on a vegetarian diet is difficult and requires a lot of planning.*
Fact: Vegetarian diets easily supply plenty of protein, without all the fat and cholesterol of meat-based diets. No complicated planning or food combining is necessary. Just eat a variety of grains, beans, vegetables and fruits each day.

Myth: *Athletes need extra protein to meet increased demands on their bodies.*
Fact: While athletes may require slightly more protein than sedentary individuals, that amount is easily met with consumption of a normal diet. The protein requirement set by the U.S. government is purposely high to cover the requirements of athletes and those performing strenuous activities. Athletes need more calories, to cover their increased energy output, and these calories should come from carbohydrate, not protein.

Putting Fat in its Place

"We have seen the enemy, and it is fat!"

Consumers frequently express concern about preservatives, artificial colorings, pesticides, hormones, and other contaminants in our food supply. Understandably, they are worried about the potentially harmful effects of these substances. Yet, by far the greatest threat in our food is not some chemical fed to animals, sprayed on fruits and vegetables, or added to processed foods. Rather, it is fat.

In the United States, most people get 40 percent of their calories each day from fat. They are amazed to learn that the majority of this fat comes from animal products— meat, dairy products, and eggs—the very foods they think of as healthful. Red meat, for example, derives about 75 percent of its calories from fat. Chicken gets 50 percent of its calories from fat; even with the skin removed 30 to 40 percent of its calories come from fat. Other animal products, including eggs and many dairy foods, supply significant amounts of fat: 50 percent of the calories in whole milk come from fat, and in cheese and eggs 70 percent of the calories are fat calories!

The health consequences of this high fat consumption are devastating. Most obvious is obesity, which affects one in every three Americans. In addition, significant research has shown that heart disease, stroke, adult onset diabetes, gallbladder disease, colon cancer, breast cancer, prostate cancer, and many other diseases are linked to high fat consumption. Research further indicates that reducing your fat intake to 30 percent of calories, as is recommended by the American Heart Association and other health agencies, does little to reduce your risk of developing these diseases. In order to have a significant impact, fat should be no more than 20 percent of your daily calories.

The easiest way to reduce your fat consumption is to reduce your intake of animal products.

With only a few exceptions (nuts, seeds, avocados, and olives), plant foods are low in fat. Grains, legumes, vegetables, and fruits get 5 to 10 percent of their calories from fat. As you replace animal foods with plant foods, your intake of fat will automatically decline, and with it, your weight and risk of disease. At the same time, your consumption of complex carbohydrate and fiber will increase. As a result, you will feel better, constipation will no longer be a problem, and you will lose excess weight without ever going hungry.

Suggestions for further decreasing your fat consumption, by reducing your use of refined fats and oils are given on the following page.

Cutting the Fat

The following techniques can help you cut the fat without sacrificing the flavor:

- **Grilling**, **baking**, and **oven-roasting** are great alternatives to frying.

- Liquid-braise vegetables such as onions, instead of sauteing them in oil. Heat approximately 1/2 cup of liquid (water, vegetable stock, wine, dry sherry) in a large skillet or pot. Add the onions (or other vegetables) and cook over high heat, stirring occasionally, until tender. This usually takes about five minutes. Then proceed with the recipe.

- The **braise-deglaze** technique allows you to actually caramelize onions (or other vegetables), bringing out all their natural flavor and sweetness with no added fat. Heat 1/2 cup of water in a skillet (non-stick works best) and add the onions. Cook over high heat until the water has evaporated and browned bits begin sticking to the pan. Add 1/4 cup of water, stirring to loosen any stuck particles, then continue cooking, stirring occasionally, until the water has again evaporated. Repeat this process until the onions are nicely browned. This will take 15 to 20 minutes.

- Avoid deep-fried foods like French fries. Try Oven Fries (page 92) instead.

- Nonstick pots and pans allow foods to be prepared with little or no added fat.

- Many cooked vegetables taste great plain, or with a bit of seasoned rice vinegar or lemon juice. Try your favorite fat-free salad dressing on cooked vegetables.

- Replace the oil called for in salad dressing recipes with seasoned rice vinegar, vegetable stock, bean cooking liquid, or with water.

- For a thicker dressing, use a cornstarch and water mixture as follows: Whisk 1 Tbsp. cornstarch with 1 cup water. Heat in a small saucepan, stirring constantly, until thick and clear. Refrigerate. Use in place of oil in any salad dressing recipe. May be kept refrigerated for up to three weeks.

- Make soup thick and creamy by adding a potato. For soups which will be pureed, simply cook and puree the potato along with the other soup ingredients. For other soups, add instant mashed potato flakes or a pureed cooked potato.

- The amount of fat in baked goods can often be reduced with no noticeable change in taste or texture. Experiment with your recipes: start by reducing the fat by half. You may have to add a bit of extra liquid to achieve the desired consistency.

- Applesauce, mashed banana, prune puree, or canned pumpkin may be substituted for part or all of the fat in many baked goods.

- Prepare pies with a single crust to reduce the fat and calories (about 100 fewer calories per serving).

Dairy Products and Eggs

I am frequently asked why some vegetarians, in addition to eliminating meat, choose not to eat dairy products and eggs. "After all, you don't have to kill the animals for milk or eggs, so what's the problem with them?" Aside from the obvious health concerns, including fat, cholesterol, hormones, antibiotics, salmonella and other bacteria, there are a number of ethical reasons for limiting or eliminating these foods.

Let's begin with dairy products. Here we need to go back to the farm and remember that in order for a cow to produce milk, she must first produce a calf. And in order to keep her milk production high, she must produce a calf every couple of years. But the calf is not permitted to partake of its mother's milk for very long. After one or two days, the calf is forcibly removed from its mother, despite heartbreaking protestations by both.

If the calf is female, she may be raised on formula to become a future member of the herd. If the calf is male, he will most likely become a veal calf. He will be locked or chained in a 2 by 4-foot slatted stall. No bedding will be provided. He cannot turn around, or stretch, or groom himself. He cannot lie down, unless he lies on his own legs. He is kept in darkness and fed an iron-deficient formula diet. Pale, tender veal comes from animals which are malnourished and whose motion is restricted. Under these conditions he becomes weak and prone to infection and disease, so antibiotics are part of his feed ration. By the time he is six months of age, he must be slaughtered or he will die of iron deficiency anemia or its complications. He is so weakened by the anemia that he cannot even walk to the truck that will transport him to the slaughterhouse. From beginning to end, his life is a nightmare. The purchase of dairy products directly supports this cycle of cruelty.

Back at the dairy barn, the calf's mother will spend six to eight years producing calves and milk. She may or may not be free to move about: more and more dairy cows are kept in confinement, chained in tiny stalls most of their lives. Leg and foot ailments caused by continual standing on concrete, as well as udder inflammation

Andy Miller '95

resulting from the use of mechanical milking machines are common. When her production begins to decline at six to eight years of age and she is no longer profitable, she will be sold for meat. Like other meat animals, she will endure the terror and brutality of transport and slaughter. Her body will be used to make bologna and other low-quality meats.

ANDY MILLER
'95

What about eggs? When we think of eggs, most of us picture the classic barnyard hen, who spends her days scratching for food and raising her brood. In reality, modern laying hens are confined to small wire cages called "battery" cages. The average wingspan of a chicken is thirty-two inches: the average battery cage is eighteen inches by twelve inches. Several hens are packed so tightly into each cage that normal movements such as stretching and grooming are impossible. Forced to stand on a wire floor with little or no movement, day in and day out, the hens' feet become deformed and may actually grow to the wire floor. To prevent the hens from pecking and injuring one another their beaks are sliced off with a hot blade. The wire cages, arranged in rows, are stacked two and three tiers high. Hens in the lower tiers are routinely defecated upon by those above. Under these conditions, hens are highly susceptible to illness so antibiotics are a routine part of the feed ration. When their egg production drops at 18 to 24 months of age the hens are shipped out for slaughter. They will become stewing hens and chicken soup.

Another little-known aspect of egg production has to do with male chicks. Hatcheries which produce hens for egg-laying operations end up with both male and female chicks. The females, of course, will become laying hens. The males, however, are not economically viable and are disposed of soon after they hatch. The sex of each chick is determined as it moves down an assembly line and the males are thrown into large plastic garbage bags where they are slowly crushed or suffocated. In some more "modern" operations the chicks are tossed into large machines which grind them alive. When you buy eggs, you are supporting this brutality.

What about free-range eggs (eggs from chickens that are not confined to cages)? One problem is that free-range egg operations get their chicks from hatcheries, so there is still the problem of the brutal disposal of the male chicks. Furthermore, free range hens, like battery hens, are culled after they are 18 months of age. If you purchase free-range eggs, you should be aware that while these chickens may have better living conditions than battery hens, their lives are still abbreviated, and they will be slaughtered under the same terrible conditions as other chickens.

You can avoid contributing to these horrors by refusing to purchase dairy products and eggs. Commercially available soy and rice milks substitute beautifully for dairy milk on breakfast cereal and in cooking. Tofu can be scrambled in place of eggs, and is also a suitable substitute for eggs in many baked goods. Margarine or oil can be used in place of butter, and several delicious non-dairy frozen desserts are available in natural food stores and many supermarkets. Finally, the recipes in this book will guide you in the preparation of delicious, cruelty-free cuisine, which is beautiful to behold, delicious to eat, and nurturing to body and soul alike.

The following books provide additional information about factory farming:

- *Old MacDonald's (Factory) Farm,* C. David Coats, Continuum Publishing, 1989.
- *Animal Factories,* Jim Mason and Peter Singer, Harmony Books, 1990.
- *Beyond Beef,* Jeremy Rifkin, Penguin Books, 1992.
- *Diet for a New America,* John Robbins, Stillpoint Publishing, 1987.
- *Modern Meat,* Orville Schell, Random House, 1985·

The following organizations are working to end the horrors of factory farming:

- *Farm Sanctuary,* P.O. Box 150, Watkins Glen, NY 19891
- *Farm Animal Reform Movement,* P.O. Box 70123, Washington, DC 20088
- *Humane Farming Association,* 1550 California St., San Francisco, CA 94109

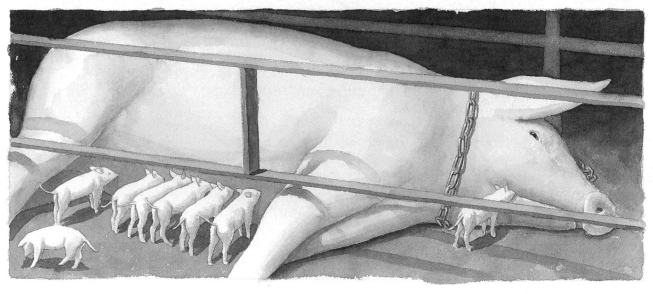

A Note About Sweeteners

I must admit to a certain puzzlement when it comes to choosing and recommending sweets and sweeteners. The best advice would be to stay away from all refined sweeteners and eat fresh fruit instead. Yet the reality is that most people love sweets and I find myself needing to "recommend" sweets and sweeteners.

Refined sweeteners, regardless of form—sugar, molasses, fructose, "raw sugar," etc.—contribute little besides calories (and of course flavor) to the diet. With the exception of blackstrap molasses (which isn't very sweet), the vitamin and mineral content of most sweeteners is so minimal as to be really insignificant. In other words, sugar is sugar is sugar. This being the case, the particular sweetener you choose is of less importance, in terms of health, than the amount you use. The real danger of sweeteners is that they tend to drive our taste buds wild, causing us to overeat the foods that contain them. Furthermore, high-sugar foods are often high-fat foods, adding to an already excessive fat intake.

A few years ago I used honey almost exclusively. However, honey is an animal product produced by bees during the spring and summer to sustain the hive through the winter. When the honey is removed for human consumption the bees lose their winter food supply. In some commercial operations sugar water is substituted to sustain the hive through the winter. In others, the bees are killed with lethal gas as winter approaches. Neither alternative is really acceptable for individuals not wishing to exploit animals.

White sugar has traditionally been avoided by ethical vegetarians and vegans because it is processed with charred bone material, a slaughterhouse by-product. The same applies to brown sugar which is actually white sugar with a bit of molasses added to it. Although the bone-char process is only used in the production of cane sugar, and much sugar in the United States is beet sugar, it is impossible to tell the difference between them unless it is specified on the package.

There are several sweeteners that may be substituted for white (or brown) sugar, that do not utilize the bone-char process. These include:
- fructose, which looks just like white sugar
- raw sugar (also called "turbinado sugar")
- granulated cane juice (Sucanat is one brand available in natural food stores)

Any of these sweeteners will work satisfactorily in the recipes in this book which specify "sugar or other sweetener."

Other sweeteners which might be used include maple syrup, brown rice syrup, corn syrup, liquid cane juice, sorghum, and barley malt. These liquids are usually interchangeable with one another as well as with honey.

Cooking with Dried Beans

Dried beans are nutritional goldmines. They supply protein, complex carbohydrate, soluble fiber, calcium, iron, and potassium, as well as other nutrients. They are delicious, very inexpensive, and easy to store.

If you're thinking that dried beans are difficult to prepare, think again. While their preparation requires a bit of advance planning—allowing time for soaking and cooking—the process is really quite simple. Rinse the beans, then soak them for 6 to 8 hours. Pour off the soaking water, add fresh water, and cook them on the stovetop, in a crockpot, or in a pressure cooker until they are tender. The amount of time this takes depends on the variety of bean.

Although soaking beans prior to cooking is not absolutely necessary, it significantly decreases their cooking time and makes them more digestible. Substances called oligosaccharides, that are not digestible by humans and may cause gas, are leached out of the beans during soaking. For this reason the soaking water is discarded and the beans are cooked in fresh water.

The following chart provides cooking guidelines for various types of beans:

Beans (1 cup dry)	Amount of water	Cooking time	Yield
black beans	3 cups	11/2 hours	21/4 cups
black-eyed peas	3 cups	1 hour	2 cups
chickpeas (garbanzos)	4 cups	2 hours	21/2 cups
great northern beans	31/2 cups	2 hours	2 cups
kidney beans	3 cups	11/2 hours	2 cups
lentils, brown	3 cups	1 hour	21/4 cups
lentils, orange	3 cups	20 minutes	2 cups
lima beans	2 cups	11/2 hours	11/2 cups
navy beans	3 cups	11/2 hours	2 cups
pinto beans	3 cups	11/2 hours	21/4 cups
soybeans	4 cups	3 hours	21/2 cups
split peas	3 cups	1 hour	21/2 cups

Beans freeze very nicely; so make extra whenever you are cooking them and freeze them in usable portions (2 cup portions are convenient) for later use.

Equipping Your Kitchen

Having the right tools will greatly increase your enjoyment of food preparation. The equipment required for preparing the recipes in this book is really quite simple, and is available fairly inexpensively in hardware stores, department stores, and cooking supply stores.

- knives—good quality knives are essential, and may be purchased at hardware or cutlery stores. Chicago Cutlery makes excellent knives which are very reasonably priced. You will need an 8 or 10-inch chef's knife, a slicing knife, a paring knife, and a serrated bread knife.

- cutting board—a wooden cutting board is the easiest to work on and is the best for your knives. Studies have shown that wooden cutting boards are just as hygienic as plastic cutting boards. Select a cutting board which is large enough to work on comfortably, but small enough to lift easily. A good size is about 12 x 15 inches.

- nonstick skillet—one of the easiest ways to reduce fat is to use a nonstick skillet. Many foods can be cooked without any added fat, and other foods can be cooked with much less fat than would otherwise be required. Look for a good-quality, heavy-duty pan. These are available in department stores, specialty cooking stores, and restaurant supply stores. Although they are not cheap, they will last a lifetime if cared for properly.

- pots and pans—you will need a large soup pot and a couple of smaller saucepans. Heavy-guage stainless steel, enamel ware, glass, or high-quality nonstick pans are all excellent choices.

- measuring cups—a set of stainless steel measuring cups in graduated sizes and a four-cup glass measuring cup should meet all your needs.

- measuring spoons

- rubber spatula—invaluable for scraping bowls and pans

- metal spatula—for turning burgers, pancakes, and braised potatoes

- large wooden or metal spoons for stirring

- glass or metal baking pans—convenient sizes are 9 x 9-inch square, 9 x 13-inch rectangular, a 9 or 10-inch pie pan, and a 5 x 9 inch bread pan.

- mixing bowls—two or three large stainless steel mixing bowls

- colander—metal or plastic, for draining pasta and for rinsing vegetables and fruits

- vegetable steamer—a metal rack or basket which enables vegetables to be cooked above (rather than in) water

Stocking Your Pantry for Healthful Eating

By keeping some basic ingredients on hand, you can prepare quick, nutritious meals at a moment's notice. Some of the items listed below are ingredients which show up frequently in recipes. Others are healthful, quick-to-prepare alternatives for those days when there just isn't time to cook. If you were to take an inventory of my pantry, here is what you would find (brand names for some items are shown in parentheses):

Dry Goods
cold breakfast cereals without added fat or sugars
hot breakfast cereals
pasta, including fettucine, spirals, lasagne
brown basmati rice
white basmati rice
quick cooking brown rice (Lundberg)
bulgur wheat
couscous
polenta
rolled oats
whole wheat flour
whole wheat pastry flour
unbleached flour
cornmeal
popcorn
dried lentils
split peas
pinto beans
raisins
instant soups: vegetarian soup cups, ramen soups
black bean flakes (Taste Adventure, Fantastic Foods)
pinto bean flakes (Taste Adventure, Fantastic Foods)
aseptically packaged reduced-fat tofu (keeps unrefrigerated for 6 months to 1 year)
vegetable broth: powder, cubes, or canned
vegetable oil spray
baking soda
baking powder

Canned foods (canned goods should be used within one year)
canned beans, including kidney, garbanzo, black, pinto, etc.
canned tomatoes, tomato sauce , tomato paste
canned pumpkin
applesauce
vegetarian soups
vegetarian baked beans (Bush's, Heinz)
vegetarian chili beans (Dennison's, Health Valley)
fat-free refried beans (Rosarita, Old El Paso, Bearitos)
vegetarian spaghetti sauce
salsa

Perishable Foods
pre-washed salad mix
pre-washed spinach
broccoli
kale or collard greens

Semi-perishable foods
yellow onions
garlic
red potatoes
russet potatoes
yams or sweet potatoes
winter squash
green cabbage
carrots
celery
apples
oranges
bananas
whole grain bread (may be frozen)
flour tortillas   (may be frozen)
corn tortillas   (may be frozen)

Frozen foods (should be used within 6 months)
apple juice concentrate
orange juice concentrate
frozen corn
frozen peas
frozen bananas
frozen berries
frozen chopped onions
frozen diced bell peppers
vegetarian hot dogs (Smart Dogs, Yves Veggie Wieners)
vegetarian burgers (Boca Burger, Natural Touch Burger by Morningstar Farms)

Seasonings and Condiments
herbs and spices: cinnamon, ginger, cloves, ground cumin, cayenne, chili powder,
                    red pepper flakes, curry powder, basil, oregano, black pepper
low-sodium soy sauce
seasoned rice vinegar
balsamic vinegar
cider vinegar
stone ground mustard
ketchup
eggless mayonnaise (Nayonaise)
unsweetened fruit preserves
molasses
maple syrup
fructose or raw sugar
salt

What to Eat When You Don't Eat Meat . . .

Breakfast Ideas
cold cereal (choose varieties with no added fat and minimal sugar)
hot cereal: oatmeal, nine-grain, etc.
bagels
toast
muffins
Whole Wheat Pancakes
Buckwheat Pancakes
Sourdough Waffles
French Toast
fresh fruit
Smoothies

Lunches and Dinners

Chili Beans
Cornbread
Mixed Greens with Piquant Dressing
Berry Cobbler

Lasagne
Herb and Onion Bread
Green Salad with Fat-free Dressing
Poached Pears

Shepherd's Pie
Basmati and Wild Rice Pilaf
Winter Squash with Peanut Sauce
Broccoli with Mustard Vinaigrette
Pumpkin Pie

Simply Wonderful Vegetable Stew
Quick and Easy Brown Bread
Green Salad with Fat-free Dressing
Banana Cake

Black Bean Bisque
Antipasto Salad
Rye Bread
Baked Apples

Neat Loaf
Mashed Potatoes & Gravy
Mixed Greens with Apples and Walnuts
Applesauce Cake

Tofu Burgers
Oven Fries
Corn on the Cob
Spinach Salad with Curry Dressing
Peach Cobbler

Pasta with Broccoli and Pinenuts
Italian Green Beans
Herb and Onion Bread
Tofu Cheesecake

Baked Beans
Braised Cabbage
Cucumber Salad
Quick and Easy Brown Bread

Split Pea Soup
Tofu Salad Sandwich
Antipasto Salad
Ginger Crinkle Cookies

Masoor Dal
Curried Mushrooms and Chickpeas
Pilau or Couscous
Chutney
Gingerbread

Lentil Barley Soup
Spinach Salad with Curry Dressing
Whole Wheat Bread
Berry Cobbler

Golden Mushroom Soup
Mixed Greens with Apples and Walnuts
Pumpkin Spice Muffins

Truly Terrific Tacos
Chili Potato Soup
Mixed Greens with Piquant Dressing
Pecan Drops

Antipasto Salad
Tomato Bisque
Sourdough French Bread
Carrot Cake

Foods Which May Be New to You

Most of the ingredients in the recipes will be familiar and widely available in grocery stores. A few which may be new to you are described below.

agar — used for thickening and gelling foods as an alternative to gelatin which is a slaughterhouse by-product; available in natural food stores and Oriental markets.

arrowroot powder — used as a substitute for cornstarch by those with allergies to corn or those desiring a less refined product; available in natural food stores.

aseptically packaged tofu — (see silken tofu)

balsamic vinegar — delicious, mellow wine vinegar available in most grocery stores.

barley malt — sweetener made from barley with a consistency slightly thicker than molasses; available in natural food stores.

basmati rice — flavorful variety of long-grain rice; brown basmati rice is less refined than white basmati rice; sold in natural food stores and many supermarkets.

bulgur — toasted, cracked wheat which cooks quickly and has a delicious, nutty flavor; sold in natural food stores and often in supermarkets as "Ala".

couscous — also called "Middle Eastern pasta;" made from the same type of wheat as other pastas, however the wheat is cracked instead of ground; sold in the grain section of many supermarkets, and in natural food stores and ethnic markets; whole wheat couscous is sold in some natural food stores.

diced chilies — refers to mildly hot chilies (like Anaheim) which are available canned or fresh. "Ortega" is a widely-sold brand. If using fresh chilies, remove the skin by charring it under a broiler then rubbing it off.

flax seeds — used as an egg substitute in baked goods. Grind and mix them with water. Excellent source of the essential fatty acid, linoleic acid.

lavash bread — Middle Eastern flatbread, similar to a very large flour tortilla. May be rolled up around a variety of fillings, or used for dipping with sauces and stews; available in some supermarkets, natural food stores, and ethnic food stores.

low-sodium baking powder—baking powder made without sodium bicarbonate; sold in natural food stores.

low-sodium soy sauce—soy sauce with reduced amounts of sodium;compare labels to get the brand that is lowest; available in most grocery stores.

mirin — sweet rice wine used in cooking; available in most grocery stores in the ethnic food section.

miso — fermented soybean paste which adds flavor and saltiness; light miso has a milder flavor, dark miso is more robust; available in natural food stores.

Nayonaise — eggless, dairyless (and therefore cholesterol-free) mayonnaise made by Nasoya; available in natural food stores.

non-dairy frozen dessert — frozen desserts made with soy milk, rice milk, or fresh fruits, containing no dairy products or eggs; "Tofutti," "Sweet Nothings," "Rice Dream," "Living Rightly," and "Nouvelle Sorbet" are several brands available in natural food stores; look for "Haagen Dazs Sorbet" and "Mocha Mix" in supermarkets.

non-dairy yogurt — cultured soymilk with a yogurt-like taste and texture. "White Wave Dairyless" and "Nancy's" are two brands which are available in a variety of flavors, including plain, from natural food stores.

nutritional yeast — adds flavor as well as nutritional value to foods; a rich source of B- vitamins (look for brands which include vitamin B-12); similar to "brewer's yeast" but better tasting; sold in natural food stores.

red pepper flakes — dried, crushed chili peppers; sold in the Mexican food or spice section of many supermarkets.

reduced-fat tofu — lower-fat tofu available in natural food stores and some supermarkets. "Mori Nu" and "White Wave" are two brands.

rice milk — mild-flavored beverage made from partially fermented rice. May be used in place of dairy milk on cereal and in most recipes. "Rice Dream" is a popular brand available in natural food stores and some supermarkets.

rice syrup — thick liquid sweetener made from brown rice; sold in natural food stores.

roasted red peppers — add flavor and color to a variety of dishes; roast your own or purchase them already roasted, packed in water, in most grocery stores.

salt-free seasoning — mixtures of herbs which provide flavor without sodium; a wide selection of brands and flavors are available in supermarkets.

seasoned rice vinegar — mild-tasting vinegar with sweet-sour flavor; excellent for salad dressings; available in most supermarkets.

seitan ("say-tan") — also called "wheat meat," seitan is a wheat product with a meaty taste and texture; it is usually marinated in soy sauce; available in the deli case of natural food stores. A dry mix for making your own seitan is made by "Knox Mountain Farm," and sold in natural food stores.

silken tofu — smooth, delicate tofu which is excellent for sauces, cream soups, and dips; special packaging permits storage without refrigeration for up to a year; refrigerate after opening. One brand, "Mori-Nu," is available in most grocery stores.

soba — Japanese buckwheat pasta, available in natural food stores, Asian markets, and many supermarkets.

soy milk — milk made from soybeans; many brands (each with its own flavor) are sold in natural food stores and supermarkets, generally in convenient aseptic packaging which does not require refrigeration until it has been opened. Soy milks are available in low-fat, fat-free, and vitamin and mineral fortified versions.

Spectrum Naturals Spread — vegetable oil spread, similar to soft margarine, but made without hydrogenated fats; sold in natural food stores.

tahini — sesame seed butter, used in Middle Eastern cooking; may be raw or toasted; available in natural food stores and many supermarkets.

tempeh — fermented soybean product, high in protein and fiber, with a more substantial texture than tofu; available in natural food stores.

textured vegetable protein (TVP) — dried granules of defatted soy flour with meaty texture when rehydrated; use in sauces, chili, and stews; available in natural food stores.

turbinado sugar — also called "raw sugar"; does not undergo the final whitening process (bone char process) of granulated sugar; available in supermarkets and natural food stores.

unbleached flour — white flour which has not been chemically whitened. Available in most grocery stores.

whole wheat pastry flour — produces lighter-textured baked goods than regular whole wheat flour; milled from soft spring wheat, it retains the bran and germ, as well as the vitamins and minerals; available in natural food stores.

BREAKFASTS

Until he extends the circle of his compassion to all living things,
man will not himself find peace.
Albert Schweitzer

Tips for Making Perfect Pancakes

- *Mix the dry ingredients in one bowl and the liquids in another. Combine them just before cooking, and stir only enough to remove any lumps.*

- *Use a good-quality nonstick skillet or griddle. Some recipes can be cooked without any fat or oil; some will require a light misting of vegetable oil spray to prevent the pancakes from sticking.*

- *Keep the cakes small—they're easier to turn.*

- *Preheat the pan so that sprinkles of water dance on it, but not so hot that it smokes.*

- *Pour a small amount of batter into the pan and let it cook until the top is bubbly and the edges look dry. Then flip the cake and cook the second side about one minute.*

- *Pancakes are best when served fresh and hot. Try them with fresh fruit and a non-dairy yogurt like White Wave Dairyless. Or serve them with fruit preserves or with syrup.*

Simple Whole Wheat Pancakes

Makes 16 3-inch pancakes

These nutritious, whole wheat pancakes are delicious with fresh fruit, fruit preserves, or maple syrup.

1	banana
1 1/4	cups soy milk or rice milk
1	tablespoon maple syrup
1	cup whole wheat pastry flour or whole wheat flour
2	teaspoons low-sodium baking powder
1/4	teaspoon salt

In a large bowl, mash the banana, then stir in the soymilk or rice milk and maple syrup. In a separate bowl, mix the flour, baking powder, and salt. Add to the banana mixture and stir until smooth.

Pour small amounts of batter onto a preheated nonstick, lightly oil-sprayed griddle or skillet and cook until the tops bubble. Turn with a spatula and cook the second side about 1 minute. Serve immediately.

Per pancake: 44 calories; 1 g protein; 8 g carbohydrate; 0 g fat; 9 mg sodium; 0 mg cholesterol

Buckwheat Pancakes

Makes about 40 3-inch pancakes

My husband and I spent our honeymoon in New England. One perfect autumn morning we stopped at a picturebook cafe for breakfast. With great anticipation we ordered their buckwheat pancakes (served with pure maple syrup, of course!). Unfortunately, the pancakes were leaden, unredeemed even by the marvelous maple syrup. We left hungry and determined to find the buckwheat pancakes of our dreams. Ironically, we found them about two years later, right in our own kitchen. The recipe, which is given below, makes 4 to 6 generous servings. It may be halved for smaller groups.

2	cups buckwheat flour
1	cup unbleached or whole wheat pastry flour
1	package active dry yeast (1 tablespoon)
1	teaspoon salt (optional)
2 1/2	cups very warm water (about 100° F)
1	teaspoon baking soda
1	tablespoon molasses
1/2	cup very warm water (about 100° F)

Preheat the oven to 200° F, then turn it off. In a large bowl mix the buckwheat and unbleached flours, the yeast, and salt. Add 2 1/2 cups of very warm water and beat until smooth. Cover and place in the oven to rise (Be sure the oven is turned off!) until very bubbly, about 1 hour. Remove from the oven.

Dissolve the soda and molasses in 1/2 cup of very warm water and add it to the buckwheat batter. Mix well, then let stand 30 minutes.

Heat a nonstick skillet or griddle. Mist it lightly with vegetable oil spray. Pour small amounts of batter onto the heated surface and cook until puffed and bubbly. Turn and cook the second side about 1 minute. Serve immediately with syrup, fruit preserves, or fresh fruit.

Per pancake: 31 calories; 1 g protein; 6 g carbohydrate; 0 g fat; 75 mg sodium; 0 mg cholesterol

Sourdough Pancakes or Waffles

Makes 16 3-inch pancakes or 8 5-inch waffles

Sourdough starter gives a wonderful, tangy flavor to these easy-to-make pancakes or waffles. Specialty food stores sell sourdough starter mixes, or better yet, get some from a friend who keeps sourdough starter.

1	**teaspoon baking soda**
2	**tablespoons maple syrup**
1	**tablespoon vegetable oil (optional)**
2	**cups sourdough starter**

In a mixing bowl, stir together the soda and maple syrup. Add the oil if you are using it, and the sourdough starter. Mix well.

For pancakes: Pour the batter onto a hot, lightly oil-sprayed nonstick griddle or skillet and cook until puffed and bubbly. Turn and cook the other side. Serve immediately with syrup, fruit preserves, or fresh fruit.

For waffles: Cook the batter in a preheated, oil-sprayed waffle iron until golden brown, 3 to 5 minutes. Serve immediately.

Per pancake (with oil): 41 calories; 1 g protein; 7 g carbohydrate; 1 g fat; 52 mg sodium; 0 mg cholesterol

Per pancake (w/o oil): 32 calories; 1 g protein; 7 g carbohydrate; 0 g fat; 52 mg sodium; 0 mg cholesterol

Per waffle (with oil): 73 calories; 2 g protein; 13 g carbohydrate; 2 g fat; 103 mg sodium; 0 mg cholesterol

Per waffle (w/o oil): 58 calories; 2 g protein; 13 g carbohydrate; 0 g fat; 103 mg sodium; 0 mg cholesterol

Oatmeal Waffles

Makes 8 5-inch waffles

I love these substantial waffles, but they're not for everyone. They are quite dense, a bit like eating oatmeal with a crunchy crust. They are quick to prepare and contain no added fat.

2	**cups rolled oats**
2	**cups water**
1	**banana**
1	**tablespoon maple syrup**
1	**teaspoon vanilla**
1/4	**teaspoon salt**

Preheat a waffle iron.

Place the rolled oats, water, banana, maple syrup, vanilla, and salt into a blender. Blend on high speed until very smooth.

Spray the waffle iron with vegetable oil spray, then pour in the batter until it nearly reaches the edges of the waffle iron. Cook for 10 minutes without lifting the lid (this time may vary slightly with different waffle irons; the important thing is not to lift the lid until the waffle is done). Serve with fresh fruit, fruit preserves, or syrup.

Note: The batter should be pourable like pancake batter. If it becomes too thick with standing, add a bit more water to achieve desired consistency.

Per waffle: 93 calories; 4 g protein; 17 g carbohydrate; 1 g fat; 67 mg sodium; 0 mg cholesterol

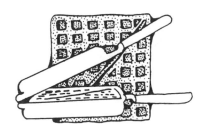

Orange French Toast

Makes 4-6 slices

French toast is quick to prepare and cholesterol-free when you make it without eggs. Vary the bread you use for different flavors and textures (cinnamon raisin is my favorite).

1	**cup soy milk or rice milk**
3	**tablespoons cornstarch**
1	**tablespoon orange juice concentrate**
1	**tablespoon maple syrup**
1	**teaspoon vanilla**
1/8	**teaspoon salt**

4-6   slices whole grain bread

Combine the soy milk or rice milk, cornstarch, orange juice concentrate, maple syrup, vanilla, and salt in a broad, flat dish and mix well. Add the bread, one slice at a time, and coat both sides with the mixture.

Preheat a nonstick skillet and mist it with a vegetable oil spray. Add the soaked bread and cook until it is golden brown, about three minutes. Turn it carefully with a spatula and cook the second side until golden brown, about 3 minutes. Serve hot with maple syrup or fruit preserves.

Per slice: 91 calories; 3 g protein; 17 g carbohydrate; 1 g fat; 110 mg sodium; 0 mg cholesterol

Scrambled Tofu

Serves 2-3

I enjoy Scrambled Tofu with English Muffins and the Braised Potatoes below. Or serve it with vegetarian sausage. A wide variety of brands are available at natural food stores and in many supermarkets (check the freezer case).

2	teaspoons toasted sesame oil
2	green onions, chopped, including tops
1/2	pound firm tofu, crumbled
1/4	teaspoon turmeric
1/4	teaspoon garlic powder or granules
1/4	teaspoon cumin
1/8	teaspoon black pepper
2	teaspoons soy sauce

Heat the oil in a nonstick skillet and sauté the onions for 3 minutes. Add the tofu, turmeric, garlic powder or granules, cumin, black pepper, and soy sauce. Cook, stirring gently for 3 to 5 minutes.

Per serving: 84 calories; 8 g protein; 5 g carbohydrate; 3 g fat; 138 mg sodium; 0 mg cholesterol

Braised Potatoes

Serves 4

These potatoes are delicious with black bean chili and spicy salsa (a real eye-opener breakfast!) or with Scrambled Tofu. Be sure to use a nonstick skillet.

4	large red potatoes
1/2	cup water
4	teaspoons soy sauce
1	onion, chopped
1	teaspoon chili powder
1/8	teaspoon black pepper

Scrub the potatoes, but do not peel. Cut into 1/4-inch thick slices and steam over boiling water until just tender when pierced with a sharp knife, about 10 minutes.

Heat 1/2 cup of water and 2 teaspoons of soy sauce in a large nonstick skillet. Add the onion and cook until soft, about 5 minutes. Add the cooked potatoes, chili powder, and remaining soy sauce. Stir gently to mix , then cook over medium heat for 5 minutes, stirring occasionally. Sprinkle with fresh ground black pepper.

Per serving: 200 calories; 6 g protein; 44 g carbohydrate; 0 g fat; 215 mg sodium; 0 mg cholesterol

Muesli

Makes about 3 cups

Muesli, which originated in Switzerland, is a mixture of uncooked grains, nuts and dried fruits. It is delicious with hot or cold soy milk or rice milk, fruit juice, or applesauce. The recipe makes about 3 cups of Muesli, which should be stored in the refrigerator.

2	**cups rolled oats**
1/4	**cup chopped almonds**
1/2	**cup chopped dried fruit (apples, figs, apricots, etc.)**
1/2	**cup raisins**

Combine all of the ingredients. Leave whole or grind in a food processor for a finer cereal. Store in an airtight container in the refrigerator.

To serve, mix with soy milk, rice milk, fruit juice, or applesauce and let stand several minutes before serving.

Per 1/2 cup: 184 calories; 6 g protein; 30 g carbohydrate; 4 g fat; 3 mg sodium; 0 mg cholesterol

Creamy Oatmeal

Makes 3 cups

This oatmeal is thinner and more porridge-like than traditional oatmeal. Once you've tried it, you may never want it any other way. Rice Dream Beverage is available in natural food stores and some supermarkets.

1	**cup rolled oats**
2 1/2	**cups Vanilla Rice Dream Beverage**

Combine the rolled oats and Rice Dream in a saucepan over medium heat. Bring to a simmer and cook 1 minute. Turn off the heat, cover the pan, and let stand 3 minutes.

Note: For thicker oatmeal, reduce the amount of Rice Dream to 2 cups.

Per cup: 194 calories; 8 g protein; 34 g carbohydrate; 3 g fat; 91 mg sodium; 0 mg cholesterol

Applesauce

Makes about 4 cups

Homemade applesauce is quite simple to prepare, and so much more flavorful than commercially prepared varieties. Cook it on the stove or in a crockpot: directions for both are given below. Serve hot or cold, as a topping for toast, pancakes, or cereal.

6	**large tart apples (gravenstein, pippins, Granny Smith, etc.)**
1/2-1	**cup undiluted apple juice concentrate**
1/2	**teaspoon cinnamon**

For chunky applesauce: peel the apples, then core and dice them into a large pan. Add enough apple juice concentrate to just cover the bottom of the pan. Cover and cook over low heat until the apples are soft. Mash slightly with a fork, if desired, then stir in the cinnamon. Serve hot or cold.

For smoother applesauce (no peeling required!): Cut the apples into quarters and remove the cores. Grind the apples, a few at a time, into small pieces in a food processor. Place in a pan with 1/2 cup of apple juice concentrate and the cinnamon. Cover and cook, stirring occasionally, over low heat until soft, about 15 minutes.

Crockpot method: Place the diced or chopped apples in a crockpot with 1/2 cup of apple juice concentrate and 1/2 teaspoon of cinnamon. Cook on high for 21/2 to 3 hours.

Per 1/2-cup: 90 calories; 0.3 g protein; 21 g carbohydrate; 0 g fat; 5 mg sodium; 0 mg cholesterol

Stewed Prunes

Makes about 2 cups

Stewed prunes are simple to prepare and a delicious source of vitamins, minerals, and fiber. Enjoy them with your breakfast, plain or with soy milk or rice milk.

1	**cup dried prunes**
1	**cup water**

Combine the prunes and water in a saucepan. Simmer gently for 20 minutes, until the prunes are soft. Serve hot or cold.

Per 1/2-cup: 129 calories; 1 g protein; 30 g carbohydrate; 0 g fat; 2 mg sodium; 0 mg cholesterol

Coffee Cake

Serves 12

This rich coffee cake, with its crumbly nut topping, is a perfect treat for that special breakfast or brunch.

1	**cup soy milk or rice milk**
1	**tablespoon vinegar**
1/3	**cup tofu**
2 1/4	**cups whole wheat pastry flour or unbleached flour**
1 1/4	**cups sugar or other sweetener**
3	**teaspoons cinnamon**
1 1/2	**teaspoons ginger**
1/2	**teaspoon salt**
1/2	**cup oil**
3/4	**cup chopped walnuts**
1	**teaspoon baking powder**
1	**teaspoon baking soda**

Preheat the oven to 350° F. Combine the soymilk, vinegar, and tofu in a blender. Blend until completely smooth.

In a large bowl mix the flour, sugar, 2 1/2 teaspoons cinnamon, ginger, salt, and oil. Work with a pastry knife, a fork or your fingers until well blended.

Transfer 1 1/4 cups of this mixture into a small bowl and mix in the walnuts and the remaining 1/2 teaspoon of cinnamon. Set aside.

To the remaining flour mixture add the baking powder and baking soda, along with the blended liquid ingredients. Mix until smooth, then spread evenly in an oil-sprayed 9 x 13-inch baking dish. Sprinkle with the reserved flour-nut mixture.

Bake 30 to 35 minutes, until a toothpick inserted in the middle comes out clean.

Per serving: 292 calories; 5 g protein; 37 g carbohydrate; 13 g fat; 167 mg sodium; 0 mg cholesterol

BREADS

&

MUFFINS

Until he extends the circle of his compassion to all living things,
man will not himself find peace.
Albert Schweitzer

Quick and Easy Brown Bread

Makes 1 loaf (about 20 slices)

This bread is similar to Boston Brown Bread, sweet and moist with no added fat or oil. It is quick to mix and requires no kneading or rising. It keeps well, makes wonderful toast, and is especially delicious with orange marmalade.

1 1/2	**cups soy milk**
2	**tablespoons cider or distilled vinegar**
2	**cups whole wheat flour**
1	**cup unbleached flour**
2	**teaspoons baking soda**
1/2	**teaspoon salt**
1/2	**cup molasses**
1/2	**cup raisins**

Preheat the oven to 325° F. Mix the soy milk with the vinegar and set aside.

In a large bowl mix the whole wheat flour, unbleached flour, soda, and salt. Add the soy milk mixture, molasses, and raisins. Stir just enough to mix. The batter will be fairly stiff and sticky. Spoon into a 5 x 9-inch oil-sprayed loaf pan and bake for one hour. Remove from the pan and place on a rack to cool.

Per slice: 111 calories; 3 g protein; 24 g carbohydrate; 0 g fat; 149 mg sodium; 0 mg cholesterol

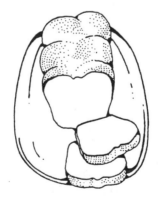

Pumpkin Raisin Muffins

These spicy muffins are light and tender with no added fat.

Makes 10 to 12 muffins

2	**cups whole wheat pastry flour**
1/2	**cup sugar or other sweetener**
1	**tablespoon baking powder**
1/2	**teaspoon baking soda**
1/2	**teaspoon salt**
1/2	**teaspoon cinnamon**
1/4	**teaspoon nutmeg**
1	**15-ounce can solid-pack pumpkin**
1/2	**cup water**
1/2	**cup raisins**

Preheat the oven to 375° F. Mix the flour, sugar, baking powder, baking soda, salt, cinnamon, and nutmeg in a large bowl. Add the pumpkin, water, and raisins. Stir until just mixed.

Lightly spray muffin cups with vegetable oil spray and fill to the top with batter. Bake 25 to 30 minutes, until the tops of the muffins bounce back when pressed. Remove from the oven and let stand 1 to 2 minutes, then remove muffins from the pan and cool on a rack. Store in an airtight container.

Per muffin: 137 calories; 3 g protein; 26 g carbohydrate; 0 g fat; 128 mg sodium; 0 mg cholesterol

Banana Oat Muffins

Makes 12 medium-sized muffins

Bananas take the place of fat in these quick and delicious muffins.

2	cups whole wheat pastry or unbleached flour
1 1/2	cups quick-cooking rolled oats or oat bran
1	teaspoon baking soda
2	ripe bananas, mashed
1 1/2	cups soy milk
2	tablespoons cider or distilled vinegar
1/2	cup molasses
1/2	cup chopped dates or raisins

Preheat the oven to 375° F. Mix the flour, oats, and baking soda in a large bowl and make a well in the center. Add the mashed bananas, soy milk, vinegar, molasses, and the dates or raisins. Stir together just enough to mix, then spoon into oil-sprayed muffin tins. Bake for 25 minutes. Remove from the oven and let stand 1 to 2 minutes. Remove the muffins from the pan and cool on a wire rack.

Per muffin: 192 calories; 5 g protein; 30 g carbohydrate; 1 g fat; 1 mg sodium; 0 mg cholesterol

Apple Oat Muffins

Makes 18 muffins

These muffins are hearty and satisfying.

1 1/2	cups whole wheat pastry flour
1 1/2	cups unbleached flour
1 1/4	cups quick-cooking rolled oats or oat bran
1	teaspoon cinnamon
1/2	teaspoon nutmeg
1/2	teaspoon salt
2 1/2	teaspoons baking soda
2	large apples, finely chopped
1	12-ounce can apple juice concentrate
1/2	cup raisins

Preheat the oven to 325° F. In a large bowl, mix the whole wheat pastry flour, unbleached flour, rolled oats, cinnamon, nutmeg, salt, and soda. Add the chopped apple along with the apple juice concentrate and raisins. Stir just enough to mix. Spoon into oil-sprayed muffin tins and bake for 25 minutes. Remove from the oven and let stand 1 to 2 minutes. Remove the muffins from the pan and cool on a wire rack.

Per muffin: 149 calories; 4 g protein; 32 g carbohydrate; 0 g fat; 180 mg sodium; 0 mg cholesterol

Cornbread

Serves 9

This delicious cornbread is made without eggs. Serve it with chili or any other spicy bean dish.

1 1/2	**cups soy milk**
1 1/2	**tablespoons vinegar**
1	**cup cornmeal**
1	**cup unbleached flour**
2	**tablespoons sugar or other sweetener**
1/2	**teaspoon salt**
1	**teaspoon baking powder**
1/2	**teaspoon baking soda**
2	**tablespoons oil**

Preheat the oven to 425° F. Combine the soy milk and vinegar and set aside.

Mix the cornmeal, unbleached flour, sugar, salt, baking powder, and baking soda in a large bowl. Add the soy milk mixture and the oil. Stir until just blended. Spread the batter evenly in an oil-sprayed 9 x 9-inch baking dish. Bake until the top is golden brown, 25 to 30 minutes. Serve hot.

Per serving: 150 calories; 3 g protein; 26 g carbohydrate; 3 g fat; 180 mg sodium; 0 mg cholesterol

Garlic Bread

Makes one loaf (about 20 slices)

The mellow flavor of roasted garlic makes delicious fat-free garlic bread.

2	**large heads garlic**
1	**baguette or loaf of French bread, sliced**
1-2	**teaspoons mixed Italian herbs (optional)**
1/4	**teaspoon salt**

Roast the whole, unpeeled heads of garlic in a 400° F oven (or toaster oven) until they feel soft when squeezed. This will take about 30 minutes. Reduce the oven temperature to 350°F.

Peel the cloves or squeeze them out of their skin, then mash them into a paste with a fork. Mix in the herbs, if desired, and salt. Spread onto the sliced bread. Wrap tightly in foil and bake for 20 minutes.

Per slice: 91 calories; 3 g protein; 18.5 g carbohydrate; 0 g fat; 179 mg sodium; 0 mg cholesterol

Making Bread with Yeast

There is nothing quite as satisfying as a perfect loaf of bread, fresh from the oven, and nothing quite as discouraging as bread which fails to rise and bake properly.

I believe that the two main causes of bread making failure are using water which is not hot enough, and not having a warm enough place for the dough to rise. The water used to make bread should be 100° F to 105° F, the same temperature as a good hot bath. If your water heater is set at 120° F, hot water from the tap will be just about ideal since it is cooled slightly when put into a measuring cup. Use a thermometer to test the water temperature until you get a feel for it.

As for a warm place for the dough to rise, I suggest the oven. Turn it on to its lowest setting to heat for one minute. **Be sure to turn it off before placing bread dough in to rise!**

Bread recipes usually specify variable amounts of flour, for example, "3-5 cups." The amount you use will vary, depending on a variety of factors including weather conditions, moisture content of the flour, and how carefully you measured the liquid. If you are making a batter bread in which the dough is not kneaded (Quick Yeast Bread, Herb and Onion Bread, English Muffin Bread), flour is added until the dough just begins to pull away from the edges of the bowl. For kneaded breads (Quick Whole Wheat Bread), the dough should feel firm, but resilient. It should not be stiff and dense. Knowing when you have added just enough flour will come with practice.

Kneading and rising are the two most important factors in determining the texture of the bread. As a rule, the more the better. You will notice in the following recipes that I have kept kneading time to a minimum and have only specified a single rising in order to save time. A lighter, finer-textured bread can be made by increasing the kneading time and by allowing the bread to rise at least one additional time.

To make a seeded bread, add 1/4 cup of seeds (sunflower seeds, poppy seeds, millet, or flax seeds) to the dough along with the first cup of flour.

To obtain a shiny crust, brush the top of the loaf with oil or a mixture of equal parts of molasses and water right after it comes out of the oven.

Quick Yeast Bread

Makes one loaf (20 slices)

This bread takes just 2 hours to make and requires no kneading. Use a heavy-duty electric mixer to mix the dough. If you mix it by hand, double the mixing time.

2½	cups unbleached or whole wheat flour (or a combination)
3	tablespoons sugar or other sweetener
2	teaspoons salt
2	packages active dry yeast (2 tablespoons)
2	cups hot water (105° F)
2	tablespoons molasses
2-3	cups of additional flour

In a large bowl, mix 2½ cups of flour with the sugar, salt, and yeast. Stir in the hot water and molasses. Beat 2 minutes with an electric mixer, scraping the bowl occasionally. With the mixer running, pour in small amounts of additional flour until the batter begins to pull away from the side of the bowl. It will be quite sticky. Continue beating for 2 more minutes at medium speed.

Cover the bowl with plastic wrap and place it in a warm place to rise until doubled, about 40 minutes. Stir the batter down and beat vigorously for 30 seconds.

Preheat the oven to 375° F. Turn the dough into a large oil-sprayed loaf pan (or two smaller ones) and let it rise in a warm place for 10 minutes. Place it in the preheated oven and bake for 40 minutes. The bread should be golden brown and sound hollow when tapped. Remove it from the pan to cool on a wire rack.

Per slice: 115 calories; 4 g protein; 24 g carbohydrate; 0 g fat; 217 mg sodium; 0 mg cholesterol

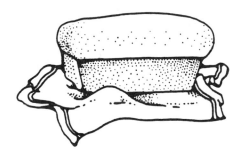

Herb and Onion Bread

Makes 1 loaf (20 slices)

The aroma of this bread as it bakes is unbelievable! Like the previous bread, it is most easily prepared with a heavy duty electric mixer. Double the mixing times if you are making it by hand.

2 1/2	cups unbleached or whole wheat flour (or a combination)
3	tablespoons sugar or other sweetener
2	teaspoons salt
2	packages active dry yeast (2 tablespoons)
1/2	teaspoon dried dill weed
1	teaspoon dried, crushed rosemary
2	cups hot water (105° F)
1/2	small onion, finely chopped
2-3	cups of additional unbleached flour

In a large bowl, mix 2 1/2 cups of flour, with the sugar, salt, yeast, and herbs. Stir in the hot water and chopped onion. Beat 2 minutes with an electric mixer, scraping the bowl occasionally.

With the mixer running, pour in small amounts of additional flour until the batter begins pulling away from the sides of the bowl. It will be very sticky. Beat 2 more minutes at medium speed.

Place the dough in a warm place to rise until doubled, about 40 minutes. At the end of this time, stir the batter down and beat vigorously for 30 seconds.

Preheat the oven to 375° F. Turn the dough into a 5 x 9-inch (or larger) oil-sprayed loaf pan, and let it rise in a warm place for 10 minutes. Bake it in the preheated oven for 40 minutes. Check it for doneness by tapping it: it should sound hollow. Remove it from the pan and cool on a wire rack.

Per slice: 109 calories; 4 g protein; 23 g carbohydrate; 0 g fat; 215 mg sodium; 0 mg cholesterol

Quick Whole Wheat Bread

Makes 1 loaf (20 slices)

This 100% whole wheat bread takes just two hours to make, from start to finish. By warming the flour and using extra yeast, only one rising is needed.

41/2	**cups whole wheat flour**
2	**tablespoons molasses**
13/4	**cup hot water (105° F)**
2	**packages active dry yeast (2 tablespoons)**
11/2	**teaspoons salt**
1/3	**cup wheat germ (optional)**

Measure the flour into a bowl and place it in a 150° F oven until warmed through, about 15 minutes.

Meanwhile, mix the molasses with the hot water in a large bowl, then sprinkle the yeast on top. Let stand until foamy, about 5 minutes. Mix in the salt and wheat germ. Add the warmed flour, 1 cup at a time, beating vigorously after each addition. When the dough begins to cling to the spoon and pull away from sides of the bowl, turn it onto a board sprinkled with flour. Knead for 5 minutes, adding enough of the remaining flour to form a smooth dough.

Shape the dough into a loaf and place it in an oil-sprayed 5 x 9-inch loaf pan. Let it rise in a warm place for 30 to 40 minutes until the dough is just above the rim of the pan. Bake in a preheated 375° F oven for 35 minutes, or until the loaf is golden brown and sounds hollow when tapped. Remove from the pan and cool on a rack.

Note: For a finer textured bread, let the dough rise in the bowl once before shaping it into a loaf, then proceed as above.

Per slice: 110 calories; 5 g protein; 21 g carbohydrate; 0 g fat; 164 mg sodium; 0 mg cholesterol

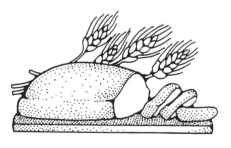

English Muffin Bread

Makes 3 loaves

This bread has a chewy texture, similar to English muffins, and makes wonderful toast. Bake it in three 1-pound coffee cans, or use three 4 x 81/2-inch bread pans.

2	tablespoons sugar or other sweetener
1	cup hot water (105° F)
2	packages active dry yeast (2 tablespoons)

cornmeal for sprinkling the pans

11/2	cups warm soy milk or rice milk
1	teaspoon salt
4-6	cups unbleached flour
1/2	teaspoon baking soda mixed with 1 tablespoon water

In a large bowl, mix the sugar and hot water, then sprinkle the yeast on top. Let stand until foamy, about 15 minutes.

Prepare three 1-pound coffee cans: Spray the cans and plastic lids with vegetable oil spray and sprinkle with cornmeal. Shake out the excess cornmeal. Note: If you don't have coffee cans, use three oil-sprayed bread pans. The bread will taste the same; it just won't be round.

Add the warmed soy milk or rice milk to the yeast mixture. Stir in the salt and 3 cups of flour. Beat well, then add the soda water.

Stir in enough additional flour to make a stiff but sticky dough. Spoon equal amounts of the dough into each can and snap on the lid. Let rise in a warm place until the lids pop off, about 45 minutes. Remove the lids. If using bread pans, let the batter rise until it is just above the tops of the pans.

Bake upright in a preheated 375° F oven for 25 to 30 minutes. Remove from the oven and let stand 5 minutes, then remove from the cans (or pans) to cool on a wire rack.

Per slice: 94 calories; 3 g protein; 20 g carbohydrate; 0 g fat; 112 mg sodium; 0 mg cholesterol

SANDWICHES

Until he extends the circle of his compassion to all living things,
man will not himself find peace.
Albert Schweitzer

Missing Egg Sandwich

Makes 4 sandwiches

Now you can enjoy the look and taste of egg salad without the cholesterol and saturated fat! Nayonaise is an eggless mayonnaise available in natural food stores.

1	cup (1/2 pound) firm tofu, mashed
2	green onions, finely chopped
1	tablespoon Nayonaise or other vegan mayonnaise
2	tablespoons pickle relish
1	teaspoon stone ground mustard
1/4	teaspoon cumin
1/4	teaspoon turmeric
1/4	teaspoon garlic powder or granules
8	slices whole wheat bread
4	lettuce leaves
4	tomato slices

Combine the mashed tofu with the green onions, Nayonaise, pickle relish, mustard, cumin, turmeric, and garlic powder or granules. Mix thoroughly.

Spread on whole wheat bread and garnish with lettuce and tomato.

Per sandwich: 197 calories;10 g protein; 29 g carbohydrate; 4 g fat; 271 mg sodium; 0 mg cholesterol

Dolphin-Friendly Mock Tuna Salad

Makes 4 sandwiches

In spite of significant publicity and legislation, the capture of tuna fish still causes injury and death to thousands of dolphins each year. This sandwich spread is truly dolphin-friendly, and tuna-friendly as well!

1	**15-ounce can garbanzo beans, drained**
1	**stalk celery, finely sliced**
1	**green onion, finely chopped**
1	**tablespoon Nayonaise or other vegan mayonnaise**
1	**tablespoon sweet pickle relish**
1/4	**teaspoon salt**
8	**slices whole wheat bread**
4	**lettuce leaves**
4	**tomato slices**

Mash the garbanzo beans with a fork or potato masher, leaving some chunks. Add the sliced celery, chopped onion, Nayonaise and relish. Add salt to taste.

Spread on whole wheat bread and top with lettuce and sliced tomatoes.

Per sandwich: 190 calories; 7 g protein; 41 g carbohydrate; 3 g fat; 241 mg sodium; 0 mg cholesterol

Tempeh Salad Sandwich

Makes 6 sandwiches

Tempeh is a soyfood that you'll find in the deli case of your natural food store. It is high in protein and fiber, and has a more substantial texture than tofu. People who are unaware of my vegetarian tendencies have often mistaken this spread for chicken salad (heaven forbid!).

8	ounces tempeh
3	tablespoons Nayonaise or other vegan mayonnaise
2	teaspoons prepared mustard
2	green onions, chopped (including green tops)
1	stalk celery, diced
1	tablespoon pickle relish
1/4	teaspoon salt
12	slices whole wheat bread
6	lettuce leaves
6	tomato slices

Steam the tempeh over boiling water for 20 minutes. Cool.

Grate the cooled tempeh and mix it with the Nayonaise, mustard, onions, celery, pickle relish, and salt. Cover and chill if time allows.

Serve on whole wheat bread with lettuce and sliced tomatoes.

Per sandwich: 247 calories; 12 g protein; 35 g carbohydrate; 6 g fat; 407 mg sodium; 0 mg cholesterol

Tofu, Lettuce, and Tomato Sandwich (TLT)

Makes 6 sandwiches

Tofu makes a perfect "short order" sandwich in this vegetarian version of the classic "BLT." Now you can enjoy all the flavor without the fat, cholesterol, or nitrates of bacon. Be sure to use a nonstick skillet to cook the tofu.

1	**pound very firm tofu**
2	**teaspoons olive oil**
1	**tablespoon soy sauce**
12	**slices whole wheat or rye bread**
1-2	**tablespoons stone ground mustard**
1-2	**tablespoons Nayonaise or other vegan mayonnaise**
6	**lettuce leaves**
6	**tomato slices**

Cut the tofu into six slices, each about 1/4-inch thick. Heat the oil in a large nonstick skillet. Add the tofu and cook over medium heat until the first side until it is golden brown, about 3 minutes. Turn and cook the second side until golden brown. Turn off the heat. Sprinkle the tofu with soy sauce, then flip it to coat both sides.

Toast the bread and spread it lightly with mustard and Nayonaise. Top with a slice of tofu, lettuce, tomato, and a second slice of bread. Serve immediately.

Per sandwich: 194 calories; 13 g protein; 22 g carbohydrate; 6 g fat; 320 mg sodium; 0 mg cholesterol

Black Bean Burritos

Makes 4 burritos

Black bean burritos are a regular meal in our house, especially when we're on the run and time is short. We have them so frequently, in fact, that I have the preparation time down to about 3 minutes! Besides being quick, they're portable: I often take a burrito with me when I travel. Dehydrated black bean flakes are available in natural food stores and some supermarkets. Two brands are "Fantastic Foods" and "Taste Adventure." Canned fat-free refried black beans are available in natural food stores.

1	cup black bean flakes mixed with 1 cup boiling water or 1 15-ounce can fat-free refried black beans
4	flour tortillas or chapatis
2	cups shredded lettuce
2	tomatoes, sliced
2	green onions, sliced
1/2	avocado, sliced (optional)
1/2	cup salsa

Mix the black bean flakes with boiling water in a small pan or bowl. Let stand until softened, 3 to 5 minutes. Or, heat the canned beans on the stove or in a microwave.

Place a tortilla in a large, ungreased skillet and heat it until it is soft and pliable.

Spread approximately 1/4 cup of black beans down the middle of the warm tortilla. Top with lettuce, tomatoes, onions, avocado, and salsa. Fold the bottom up, then starting on one side, roll the tortilla around the filling.

Per burrito: 182 calories; 8 g protein; 34 g carbohydrate; 1 g fat; 63 mg sodium; 0 mg cholesterol

Garbanzo Rollups

Makes 6 to 8 rollups

Rollups are a complete meal in an edible wrapper. They are easily portable, making them perfect for lunches or picnics. In this recipe, a delicious garbanzo paté is rolled with brown rice and salad greens. The garbanzo paté can be quickly prepared in a food processor or by hand. Directions are given for both.

2	**garlic cloves**
1	**15-ounce can of garbanzo beans**
2	**tablespoons tahini (sesame seed butter)**
2	**tablespoons lemon juice**
1/4	**teaspoon cumin**
1/4	**teaspoon paprika**
1/4	**teaspoon salt**
2	**cups cooked brown rice (see page 96)**
6-8	**flour tortillas or chapatis**
3	**cups (approximately) mixed salad greens or torn leaf lettuce**
1	**cup chopped cilantro (optional)**

Place the garlic in a food processor and chop it finely. Drain the beans, reserving the liquid, then add them to the food processor along with the tahini, lemon juice, cumin, paprika, and salt. Process until very smooth; the mixture should be moist and spreadable. If it is too dry add some of the reserved bean liquid to achieve a spreadable consistency.

To prepare the filling by hand: drain the beans, reserving the liquid, and mash them until they are very smooth. Crush the garlic and add it to the beans, along with the tahini, lemon juice, cumin, paprika, and salt. Mix well. Thin to a spreadable consistency with reserved bean liquid if needed.

To assemble the rollups: Spread a layer of paté down the center of a tortilla and top it with some of the cooked brown rice (1/4 to 1/2 cup) and salad greens. Fold the top and bottom edges of the tortilla toward the center about one inch, then begin on one side and roll the tortilla firmly around the filling.

Per serving: 270 calories; 10 g protein; 47 g carbohydrate; 4 g fat; 265 mg sodium; 0 mg cholesterol

Broiled Tofu

Makes 6 slices

Broiled tofu makes a delicious snack or sandwich. It can also be cut into pieces and added to salads, soups, or stir-fried vegetables.

1	**pound firm, fresh tofu**
1/2	**cup soy sauce**
1/2	**teaspoon garlic powder or granules**
1/2	**teaspoon ginger**
1/8	**teaspoon cayenne**
1/8	**teaspoon black pepper**

Begin by pressing the tofu. Slice it into 1/4-inch thick pieces. Arrange the slices on a baking sheet and cover them with a clean dish towel. Cover this with another cookie sheet (or similar flat object), and top this with about 5 pounds weight (canned food works well). Let stand at least 30 minutes. This will squeeze the excess water out of the tofu, making it even firmer.

Mix the soy sauce and spices for the marinade.

Place the pressed tofu slices in a single layer in a large baking dish, then pour the marinade over it. Refrigerate and marinate at least 2 hours.

Place the tofu slices on a nonstick baking sheet on the top rack of the oven, and broil until browned, 3 to 5 minutes. Turn the pieces over and cook the second side.

Per slice: 81 calories; 10 g protein; 6 g carbohydrate; 2 g fat; 400 mg sodium; 0 mg cholesterol

SALADS

&

SALAD DRESSINGS

Until he extends the circle of his compassion to all living things,
man will not himself find peace.
Albert Schweitzer

The Great New Greens

When I was growing up, a green salad meant iceberg lettuce with a few slices of tomato and cucumber, drowned in Thousand Island Dressing. Fortunately, that has changed. Most supermarkets now offer wide selections of salad greens, as varied in flavor as they are in appearance. Even better, many stores now sell mixes of these greens, prewashed and ready to use. Following is a list of some of the wonderful new greens.

Arugula (rocket or roquette). Bright green leaves are deeply serrated and have a spicy, mustard-like flavor. Delicious with milder tasting greens like butter lettuce and romaine.

Belgian endive (French endive or witloof chicory). Leaves are firm and slender forming elongated, heads that are white with pale yellow tips. The leaves are crisp and pleasantly bitter.

Chicory (curly endive). Chicory has a pleasantly bitter taste. The coarser, darker outside leaves are more strongly flavored than the inside leaves.

Baby Chicory (frisee). Softer texture and milder flavor than mature chicory.

Escarole. Outer leaves are broad and dark green; interior leaves are lighter and more tender. Slightly bitter flavor compliments loose-leaf lettuces.

Radicchio (red chicory, Italian chicory). Leaves form small, tight round heads that are red and white. It has a pleasant, slightly bitter taste, similar to chicory.

Watercress. Small rounded leaves have a spicy, peppery flavor.

Leaf lettuce. Loose leaf lettuces provide color, flavor, and texture, as well as significantly more nutritional value than iceberg lettuce.

   Butter lettuces, including Bibb, Boston, and limestone. These lettuces form loose heads and the very tender leaves have a faint, almost buttery taste.

   Green leaf. Leaves are tender and crisp with delicate flavor.

   Red leaf. Mild-flavored leaves are tender and colorful: red to bronze-tinged.

   Romaine or Cos. Mild flavor and a crunchiness which holds up well under heavy dressings.

Making Salad Dressings without Fat

Most salad dressings are between 90 and 95 percent fat. Adding more than a few teaspoons of these dressings to a salad turns an otherwise healthful meal into a high fat meal. There are a growing number of commercial alternatives to high fat salad dressings available in grocery and health food stores, but read the labels carefully.

If you are interested in making your own fat-free dressing, the simplest modification is to leave the oil out of the recipe and substitute an equal amount of seasoned rice vinegar, water, or vegetable stock. The dressing won't be as thick as you're used to, but the taste will be fine.

To make a thicker dressing, a cornstarch or arrowroot mixture may be used as a thickener in place of the oil. Whisk 1 cup of water and 1 tablespoon of cornstarch together in a small saucepan. Bring to a simmer over medium heat and cook until the mixture is clear and thickened. Allow to cool, then store in the refrigerator. This mixture may be substituted directly for the oil in any salad dressing recipe.

Seasoned rice vinegar and balsamic vinegar also make tasty salad dressings. Use them plain or in combination with other ingredients. Both are available in most grocery stores.

Fat-free Salad Dressing

Makes 1/2 cup

Seasoned rice vinegar makes a simple, delicious dressing for salads and cooked vegetables. It will keep in the refrigerator for 2 to 3 weeks.

1/2	**cup seasoned rice vinegar**
1-2	**teaspoons stone ground or Dijon mustard**
1	**garlic clove, pressed or crushed**

Whisk all the ingredients together. Store in a lidded jar or airtight plastic container.

Per tablespoon: 14 calories; 0 g protein; 3 g carbohydrate; 0 g fat; 310 mg sodium; 0 mg cholesterol

Spinach Salad with Curry Dressing

Serves 6 to 8

This wonderful spinach salad is a happy marriage of flavors and textures. It is especially easy to make when you use prewashed spinach, available in the produce departments of most supermarkets.

1/3	**cup peanuts**
1	**tablespoon sesame seeds**
1	**bunch fresh spinach, washed or 1/2 bag prewashed spinach**
1	**tart green apple, diced**
2	**green onions, thinly sliced, including green tops**
1/4	**cup sultana or golden raisins**
3	**tablespoons seasoned rice vinegar**
3	**tablespoons frozen apple juice concentrate**
2	**teaspoons stone ground or Dijon mustard**
1	**teaspoon soy sauce**
1/2	**teaspoon curry powder**
1/4	**teaspoon black pepper**

Spread the peanuts and sesame seeds in an oven-proof pan and bake at 375°F for 10 to 15 minutes. Cool.

Combine the spinach with the apple, onions, and raisins in a large salad bowl. Add the cooled peanuts and sesame seeds.

Whisk the vinegar, apple juice concentrate, mustard, soy sauce, curry powder, and black pepper together in a small bowl. Pour over the salad and toss to mix just before serving.

Per serving: 99 calories; 3 g protein; 12 g carbohydrate; 4 g fat; 102 mg sodium; 0 mg cholesterol

Chinese Noodle Salad

Serves 8

This delicious salad is easy to prepare and keeps well. Ramen soup is available in a variety of flavors at natural food stores and in the health food section of many supermarkets. It contains dry noodles and a packet of seasoning. Be sure to select a variety in which the noodles are baked instead of fried, and be sure the seasonings do not contain meat or other animal products.

1	**medium head green cabbage, finely shredded (about 8 cups)**
1/2	**cup slivered almonds**
1/4	**cup sesame seeds**
3-4	**green onions, thinly sliced or** 1/4 **cup finely chopped red onion**
1	**package vegetarian ramen soup (any flavor)**
1	**tablespoon toasted sesame oil**
1/3	**cup seasoned rice vinegar**
2	**tablespoons sugar or other sweetener**
1/2	**teaspoon black pepper**

fresh cilantro (optional)

Place the shredded cabbage in a large salad bowl.

Toast the almonds and sesame seeds in an ovenproof dish in a 375° F oven (or toaster oven) for 8 to 10 minutes, until lightly browned and fragrant. Add to the shredded cabbage, along with the onions. Coarsely crush the uncooked ramen noodles and add them to the salad.

Empty the packet of seasoning mix into a small bowl or jar, then stir in the sesame oil, seasoned rice vinegar, sugar, and pepper. Mix thoroughly and pour over the salad. Toss to mix, then allow to stand 30 minutes in order for the noodles to soften. Garnish with fresh cilantro just before serving, if desired.

Per serving: 101 calories; 2 g protein; 13 g carbohydrate; 4 g fat; 279 mg sodium; 0 mg cholesterol

Aztec Salad

Serves 8 to 10

This salad is a true celebration of color and flavor. It may be made in advance, and keeps well for several days. If you are a cilantro lover, you may want to increase the amount.

2	15-ounce cans black beans
1/2	cup finely chopped red onion
1	green bell pepper, diced
1	red or yellow bell pepper, diced
2	tomatoes, diced
2	cups frozen corn, thawed
3/4	cup chopped fresh cilantro (optional)
2	tablespoons seasoned rice vinegar
2	tablespoons apple cider or distilled vinegar
1	lime or lemon, juiced
2	garlic cloves, minced
2	teaspoons cumin
1	teaspoon coriander
1/2	teaspoon crushed red pepper flakes

Drain and rinse the beans and place them in a large salad bowl with the onion, peppers, tomatoes, corn, and cilantro. In a small bowl combine the vinegars, lemon or lime juice, garlic, cumin, coriander, and red pepper flakes. Pour over the salad and toss gently to mix.

Per serving: 143 calories; 7 g protein; 28 g carbohydrate; 0 g fat; 117 mg sodium; 0 mg cholesterol

Pasta Salad

Serves 8 to 10

This fat-free pasta salad is delicious hot or cold.   It is prepared with water-packed artichokes which are available in most supermarkets.

8	**ounces pasta spirals (about 3 cups uncooked)**
1	**cup finely chopped red onion**
1	**jar water-packed artichoke hearts, drained and quartered**
2	**cups small button mushrooms (about 1/3 pound), cleaned**
1/4	**cup cider vinegar**
1/3	**cup seasoned rice vinegar**
1	**lemon, juiced**
2	**teaspoons stone ground or Dijon mustard**
1/4	**cup chopped green onions**
1	**garlic clove**
1	**teaspoon basil**
1/2	**teaspoon oregano**
1/2	**teaspoon salt**
1/4	**teaspoon black pepper**
3	**tablespoons water**
3	**tablespoons fresh parsley, chopped**
1	**small red bell pepper, diced**

Cook the pasta in boiling water until it is just tender. Rinse with cold water, drain, and place into a large bowl. Add the chopped red onion, quartered artichoke hearts, and the mushrooms.

In a blender, combine the vinegars, lemon juice, mustard, green onions, garlic, basil, oregano, salt, black pepper, and water. Process until smooth.

Just before serving, add the dressing to the salad, along with the chopped parsley and diced red bell pepper. Toss gently to mix.

Note: If leftover pasta salad becomes dry, make a bit more of the dressing, or toss it with any good vinaigrette you have on hand.

Per serving: 70 calories; 2 g protein; 14 g carbohydrate; 0.2 g fat; 387 mg sodium; 0 mg cholesterol

Thai Noodle Salad

Serves 8

This colorful salad is substantial enough to be a meal in itself. It is made with udon, a Japanese pasta similar to spaghetti, available in natural food stores, Asian food stores, and in the ethnic foods section of many supermarkets. If you are unable to find udon, use spaghetti instead.

6	**ounces uncooked udon or spaghetti**
1	**tablespoon toasted sesame oil**
1/2	**pound asparagus**
1/2	**bunch broccoli**
1/2	**red bell pepper, cut into thin strips**
3	**green onions, finely chopped**
1	**cup bean sprouts**
1/3	**cup peanut butter**
1/4	**cup seasoned rice vinegar**
2	**tablespoons soy sauce**
1	**tablespoon dry sherry**
1/8	**teaspoon cayenne**
2	**teaspoons finely minced fresh ginger**
1	**large garlic clove, minced**

chopped fresh cilantro

Cook the udon (or spaghetti) in a large pot of boiling water until it is just tender. Drain and rinse under cold water. Toss with the sesame oil and set aside.

Snap the tough ends off the asparagus and cut it into 1-inch pieces. Cook in a pot of boiling water for 1 minute then plunge into a bowl of ice water to chill. Drain. (Save the pot of boiling water for cooking the broccoli). Separate the broccoli into bite-size florets. Peel the stems and cut into 1/2-inch pieces. Cook in boiling water until tender-crisp, 1 to 2 minutes. Chill in ice water. Drain. Cut the bell pepper into thin inch-long strips; finely chop the green onions, including the tops; freshen the bean sprouts by plunging them into ice water then draining them.

Whisk the peanut butter together with vinegar, soy sauce, sherry, cayenne, ginger, and garlic.

In a large bowl, combine the noodles and vegetables, then add the dressing. Toss gently to mix. Top with chopped cilantro if desired.

Per serving: 177 calories; 7 g protein; 21 g carbohydrate; 6 g fat; 308 mg sodium; 0 mg cholesterol

Mixed Greens with Apples and Walnuts

Serves 6 to 8

This simple salad is delicious and incredibly easy to prepare, especially if you use one of the prewashed salad mixes available in most supermarkets.

6	**cups salad mix or washed and torn leaf lettuce**
1	**large tart green apple**
1/3	**cup walnuts, coarsely chopped**
3-4	**tablespoons seasoned rice vinegar**

Place the salad mix or torn leaf lettuce into a bowl. Core and dice the unpeeled apple and add it to the greens along with the walnuts. Pour seasoned rice vinegar over the salad and toss to mix.

Per serving: 48 calories; 0.5 g protein; 6 g carbohydrate; 2 g fat; 115 mg sodium; 0 mg cholesterol

Chinese Cabbage with Citrus and Tahini Dressing

Serves 6

If you've never tried Chinese cabbage (also called "Napa cabbage") you'll be delighted with its crisp texture and mild flavor.

1	**small Chinese or Napa cabbage**
2	**satsuma tangerines, peeled and divided into segments**
	or 1 15-ounce can mandarin oranges, drained
1/4	**cup tahini**
1	**garlic clove, crushed**
1	**tablespoon lemon juice**
1	**tablespoon soy sauce**
1	**tablespoon cider vinegar**
1	**tablespoon seasoned rice vinegar**

Cut the cabbage into very fine shreds until you have about 5 cups. Place it in a salad bowl with 2/3 of the tangerine or orange segments.

Mix the tahini, garlic, lemon juice, soy sauce, cider vinegar, and seasoned rice vinegar in a small bowl, stirring with a fork until smooth. The dressing will be quite thick, but will thin as soon as it is added to the salad. Add the dressing to the salad and toss to mix. Garnish with reserved citrus slices.

Per serving: 100 calories; 3 g protein; 12 g carbohydrate; 4 g fat; 174 mg sodium; 0 mg cholesterol

Warm Red Cabbage Salad

Serves 6

Red cabbage is barely cooked, then tossed with crisp apples and toasted walnuts. So good! To avoid last-minute frenzy, do all the cutting, coring and dicing, before you start cooking.

1/3	**cup walnuts, coarsely chopped**
2	**tablespoons olive oil**
1/4	**cup balsamic vinegar**
1	**medium red onion, thinly sliced**
1	**garlic clove, minced**
1	**small red cabbage, thinly sliced (about 6 cups)**
1/4	**teaspoon dried marjoram or 1 teaspoon fresh marjoram**
1	**tart green apple, diced**
1/4	**cup raspberry vinegar or balsamic vinegar**
2	**tablespoons chopped parsley**
1/2	**teaspoon salt**
1/8	**teaspoon black pepper**

Toast the walnuts in a 350° F oven (or toaster oven) for 10 minutes.

Heat the oil and 1/4 cup of balsamic vinegar in a large skillet. Add the onion and garlic and cook 3 minutes.

Add the cabbage and marjoram. Cook, turning gently, until the cabbage is just wilted and the color has changed from purple to bright pink, about 5 minutes.

Remove from the heat and add the apple, additional vinegar, parsley, salt, and pepper. Toss to mix.

Per serving: 136 calories; 3 g protein; 12 g carbohydrate; 8 g fat; 189 mg sodium; 0 mg cholesterol

Mixed Greens Salad with Piquant Dressing

Serves 6

Prewashed mixes of salad greens are available in most supermarkets and natural food stores. These are as flavorful as they are attractive, and stand well on their own, with just a touch of dressing. Other vegetables can be added for additional flavor and nutrition, as the following recipe suggests.

1/2	**red or yellow bell pepper, seeded and sliced**
2	**red or yellow tomatoes, sliced**
1/2	**cucumber, peeled and thinly sliced**
6	**cups prewashed salad mix**
1/4	**cup seasoned rice vinegar**
2	**tablespoons ketchup**
1	**teaspoon stone ground mustard**
1	**garlic clove, pressed or crushed**
1/2	**teaspoon paprika**
1/4	**teaspoon oregano**
1/8	**teaspoon ground cumin**

Combine the bell pepper, tomatoes, cucumber, and salad mix in a large bowl.

In a small bowl mix the vinegar, ketchup, mustard, garlic, paprika, oregano, and cumin. Pour 2 to 3 tablespoons over the salad and toss to mix. Refrigerate remaining dressing for later use.

Per serving: 20 calories; 0.2 g protein; 4 g carbohydrate; 0 g fat;160 mg sodium; 0 mg cholesterol

Antipasto Salad

Serves 6 to 8

The vegetables in this salad are steamed until they are just tender, then marinated in a tangy vinaigrette. This salad may be served hot or cold.

4	**medium red potatoes, scrubbed**
2	**carrots, peeled**
11/2	**cups fresh green beans**
1/2	**head cauliflower, washed and broken into florets**
1	**cup green peas, fresh or frozen**
1	**red bell pepper, sliced**
1/4	**cup balsamic or cider vinegar**
2	**tablespoons seasoned rice vinegar**
2	**tablespoons lemon juice**
2	**garlic cloves, pressed or crushed**
2	**teaspoons stone ground or Dijon mustard**
1/2	**teaspoon salt**
1/4	**teaspoon black pepper**

Cut the potatoes into 1-inch cubes. Cut the carrots on the diagonal into 1/2-inch thick pieces. Steam over boiling water until just tender, about 10 minutes.

Trim the green beans and cut them into one-inch pieces. Steam over boiling water until just tender, 7 to 10 minutes.

Break the cauliflower into florets and steam until just tender, about 8 minutes.

Gently combine all the vegetables, including the peas and bell pepper in a salad bowl.

In a small bowl or jar, mix the vinegars, lemon juice, garlic, mustard, salt, and pepper. Pour over the vegetables and toss gently. Serve immediately or refrigerate until thoroughly chilled.

Per serving: 162 calories; 4 g protein; 36 g carbohydrate; 0 g fat; 270 mg sodium; 0 mg cholesterol

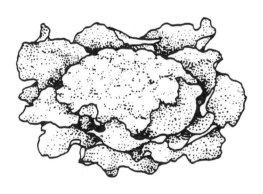

Tabouli

Serves 8

Tabouli is a traditional Middle Eastern salad made with bulgur and seasoned with lemon, parsley, mint, and garlic. I know this will sound like heresy, but I never particularly liked tabouli until I left the mint out by accident one time. Then it tasted great! So now I always make it without mint. I include the mint in this recipe as an optional ingredient for those who enjoy it.

1	**cup uncooked bulgur**
2	**cups boiling water**
2	**medium tomatoes, diced**
1/2	**cup chopped green onions (use the tops too)**
1/2	**cucumber, peeled and diced**
1/2	**cup parsley, finely chopped**
3	**tablespoons fresh mint leaves, finely chopped (optional)**
1/4	**cup lemon juice**
1	**tablespoon olive oil**
1	**garlic clove, pressed or crushed**
1/2-1	**teaspoon salt**

Put the bulgur in a large bowl and pour the boiling water over it. Cover and let stand until tender, about 25 minutes. Drain off any excess liquid and use a fork to fluff the bulgur.

Add the tomatoes, green onions, cucumber, parsley, mint (if you like it!), lemon juice, olive oil, garlic, and salt. Toss gently to mix. Chill before serving if time allows.

Per serving: 107 calories; 3 g protein; 19 g carbohydrate; 2 g fat; 271 mg sodium; 0 mg cholesterol

Three Bean Salad

Serves 8

This three bean salad is flavorful with no added fat. Serve it plain, or as an addition to green salads.

1	**15-ounce can kidney beans, drained**
1	**15-ounce can garbanzo beans, drained**
1	**15-ounce can green beans, drained**
1/2	**small red onion, finely chopped**
1/4	**cup finely chopped fresh parsley**
1/2	**cup cider vinegar**
2	**tablespoons seasoned rice vinegar**
2	**garlic cloves, pressed or crushed**
1/2	**teaspoon each: basil, oregano, and marjoram**
1/4	**teaspoon black pepper**
1/2	**teaspoon salt**

Toss the drained beans with the chopped onion and parsley in a salad bowl. In a small bowl, mix the vinegars, garlic, basil, oregano, marjoram, and pepper. Add to the beans and toss to mix. Add salt to taste. If possible, chill before before serving.

Per serving: 141 calories; 7 g protein; 26 g carbohydrate; 1 g fat; 140 mg sodium; 0 mg cholesterol

Cucumber Salad

Serves 6

This is a lovely cool salad for hot summer days. It is quick to make, has no added fat, and tastes great!

3	**large cucumbers, peeled if they are waxed**
2	**large tomatoes**
1/2	**small red onion**
1/2	**teaspoon basil**
1/2	**teaspoon dill weed**
1/4	**teaspoon black pepper**
1	**tablespoon chopped fresh parsley**
3-4	**tablespoons apple cider vinegar**

Slice the cucumbers in half lengthwise and scoop out the seeds with a spoon. Cut the cucumber into bite-sized pieces. Dice the tomatoes, and finely chop the red onion. Toss the vegetables together in a salad bowl, then sprinkle with basil, dill, black pepper, and fresh parsley. Add the vinegar and toss to mix. Chill before serving.

Per serving: 35 calories; 1 g protein; 7 g carbohydrate; 0 g fat; 7 mg sodium; 0 mg cholesterol

SAUCES
&
SPREADS

Until he extends the circle of his compassion to all living things,
man will not himself find peace.
Albert Schweitzer

Black Bean Sauce

Serves 6

Black bean sauce is quick and easy to prepare. Try it on broccoli, baked potatoes, or pasta.

1	**15-ounce can black beans, drained**
1/2	**cup roasted red pepper**
2	**tablespoons lemon juice**
2	**tablespoons tahini (sesame seed butter)**
1/2	**teaspoon chili powder**
1/4	**teaspoon cumin**
1/4	**teaspoon coriander**
1/4	**cup chopped fresh cilantro**

Puree all of the ingredients in a food processor or blender until very smooth.

Per serving: 126 calories; 6 g protein; 19 g carbohydrate; 2 g fat; 105 mg sodium; 0 mg cholesterol

Hummus

Makes 2 cups

Hummus is a creamy garbanzo paté that makes a delicious sandwich spread, or serve it as a dip with fresh vegetables or wedges of pita bread.

2	**garlic cloves**
1	**tablespoon finely chopped parsley**
1	**15-ounce can garbanzo beans**
3	**tablespoons tahini (sesame seed butter)**
2	**tablespoons lemon juice**
1/4	**teaspoon cumin**
1/4	**teaspoon paprika**
1/4	**teaspoon salt**

Place the garlic and parsley in a food processor and chop into very fine pieces. Drain the beans, reserving the liquid. Add the beans to the food processor along with the tahini, lemon juice, cumin, paprika, and salt. Process until very smooth. The mixture should be moist and spreadable. If it is too dry, add some of the reserved bean liquid to achieve the desired consistency.

Per serving: 182 calories; 7 g protein; 31 g carbohydrate; 3 g fat; 128 mg sodium; 0 mg cholesterol

Creamy Cucumber Dip

Serves 6

Serve this cool, creamy dip with wedges of fresh pita bread or with the pita chips in the following recipe.

2	cucumbers
1/4	cup finely sliced red onion
1	pound firm tofu
31/2	tablespoons lemon juice
2	garlic cloves, peeled
1/2	teaspoon salt
1/4	teaspoon coriander
1/4	teaspoon cumin

pinch cayenne

Peel, seed, and grate the cucumbers. Let stand 10 minutes, then squeeze to remove any excess liquid. Place in a mixing bowl with the red onion.

In a blender, combine the tofu, lemon juice, garlic, salt, coriander, cumin, and cayenne. Blend until completely smooth, then pour over the cucumbers and mix well. Transfer to a serving dish and chill 2 to 3 hours.

Per serving: 64 calories; 6 g protein; 6 g carbohydrate; 2 g fat; 139 mg of sodium; 0 mg cholesterol

Pita Chips

Makes 36 chips

6	pieces whole wheat pita bread
1-2	teaspoons olive oil

garlic powder or granules
chili powder
paprika
salt

Preheat the oven to 350° F. Brush the tops of the pita breads very lightly with olive oil then sprinkle with garlic powder or granules, chili powder, paprika, and salt. Cut each piece into 6 triangular wedges and spread in a single layer on two baking sheets.

Bake until very crispy, 20 to 25 minutes. Remove from oven and cool on a rack.

Per chip: 26 calories; 1 g protein; 5 g carbohydrate; 0 g fat; 81 mg of sodium; 0 mg cholesterol

Mushroom and Almond Paté

Makes about 2 cups

Serve this paté with crackers or fresh sliced baguette.

1	cup almonds
2	teaspoons olive oil
1	small onion, finely chopped
1	garlic clove, minced
31/2	cups sliced mushrooms
3/4	teaspoon thyme leaves
3/4	teaspoon salt
1/8	teaspoon black pepper

Toast the almonds in a 375° F oven until lightly browned, about 10 minutes. Cool.

Heat the olive oil in a skillet and sauté the onion and garlic 3 minutes. Add the mushrooms, thyme, salt, and black pepper and cook until the mushrooms are browned and any liquid has evaporated.

Use a food processor to grind the almonds into a paste. Add the mushroom mixture and continue to process until smooth. Chill before serving.

Per tablespoon: 32 calories; 1 g protein; 2 g carbohydrate; 2 g fat; 50 mg sodium; 0 mg cholesterol

Tahini Dip

Makes about 1 cup

This dip is delicious with fresh vegetables or wedges of pita bread. It can also be thinned with a small amount of water and used as a salad dressing. Tahini (sesame seed butter) is a traditional ingredient in Middle Eastern cooking. It adds flavor and body to sauces, salad dressings, and spreads, and is a rich source of calcium. Look for tahini in natural food stores, ethnic markets, and supermarkets.

1/2	cup tahini (sesame seed butter)
2	tablespoons lemon juice
2	tablespoons soy sauce
2	tablespoons vinegar
2	garlic cloves, pressed or crushed

Combine the tahini, lemon juice, soy sauce, vinegar, and garlic in a mixing bowl, then mix until smooth with a fork or whisk. Transfer to a serving bowl and place it on a platter surrounded with fresh vegetables or wedges of pita bread.

Per tablespoon: 46 calories; 1 g protein; 3 g carbohydrate; 3 g fat; 78 mg sodium; 0 mg cholesterol

Salsa Fresca

Makes about 6 cups

This salsa is fresh and chunky. I have purposely made it quite mild, trusting that if you want it hotter you'll know to add more crushed red pepper flakes, cayenne, or some chopped fresh jalapeños.

4	**cups chopped tomatoes**
1	**small onion, finely chopped**
1	**bell pepper, finely chopped**
4	**garlic cloves, minced**
1	**cup chopped cilantro leaves**
1	**15-ounce can tomato sauce**
2	**tablespoons cider vinegar**
1 1/2	**teaspoons cumin**
1/2	**teaspoon crushed red pepper flakes (add more for a hotter salsa)**

Combine all the ingredients in a mixing bowl and stir to mix. Let stand 1 hour before serving. Salsa will keep in the refrigerator about 2 weeks. It also freezes well.

Per tablespoon: 5 calories; 0 g protein; 1 g carbohydrate; 0 g fat; 2 mg sodium; 0 mg cholesterol

Simple Marinara

Makes about 4 cups

Marinara doesn't get any easier. . . unless you buy it ready-made! Use this simple, tasty sauce with manicotti, lasagne, or any other pasta dish.

1/2	**cup red or white wine or water**
1	**onion, chopped**
4	**garlic cloves, crushed**
1	**28-ounce can crushed or ground tomatoes**
1	**tablespoon mixed Italian herbs**
1	**tablespoon apple juice concentrate**
1/4	**teaspoon black pepper**

Heat the wine or water in a large pot, then add the onion and garlic and cook until soft, about 5 minutes.

Add the tomatoes, herbs, apple juice concentrate, and black pepper. Simmer 20 minutes.

Per 1/2 cup: 50 calories; 2 g protein; 8 g carbohydrate; 0 g fat; 33 mg sodium; 0 mg cholesterol

Simple Peanut Sauce

Makes 1 cup

Peanut sauce is quick to make and delicious with cooked vegetables or with pasta.

1/3	cup peanut butter
1/2	cup hot water
1	tablespoon soy sauce
1	tablespoon vinegar (cider or seasoned rice)
2	teaspoons sugar
2	garlic cloves, minced
1/4	teaspoon ginger
1/8	teaspoon cayenne

Whisk all the ingredients together in a small saucepan, then heat gently until the sauce is smooth and slightly thickened. Add more water if the sauce becomes too thick.

Per tablespoon: 38 calories; 1 g protein; 2 g carbohydrate; 3 g fat; 38 mg sodium; 0 mg cholesterol

Apple Chutney

Makes about 3 cups

Chutney is a spicy relish that is served as a condiment with Indian meals. This simple chutney is made with apples. It will keep in the refrigerator for several weeks, and also freezes for longer storage.

3	large tart green apples (about 1 1/2 pounds)
1	cup cider vinegar
1	cup sugar or other sweetener
1	large garlic clove, minced
1	tablespoon minced ginger root or 1/2 teaspoon ginger powder
1/2	cup orange juice
1	teaspoon each: cinnamon and cloves
1/2	teaspoon salt
1/4	teaspoon cayenne (or more to taste)

Core and coarsely chop the apples. Combine them with all the remaining ingredients in a saucepan. Bring to a simmer and cook uncovered, stirring occasionally until most of the liquid is absorbed, about 1 hour.

Per tablespoon: 22 calories; 0 g protein; 5 g carbohydrate; 0 g fat; 21 mg sodium; 0 mg cholesterol

SOUPS
&
STEWS

*Until he extends the circle of his compassion to all living things,
man will not himself find peace.*
Albert Schweitzer

A Few Words About Soup

Homemade soups are easy to make and even easier to reheat. They can be prepared without fat, and practically cook themselves, whether on the stove or in a crockpot. Serve them with bread and a green salad for a satisfying and nutritious meal.

You will notice that several of the recipes give the option of using water or vegetable stock. If you have vegetable stock on hand, use it for the extra flavor it imparts.

Speaking of vegetable stock, there are a number of commercial vegetarian soup stocks, usually in powdered form, available in natural food stores. You can also find canned vegetable stock, made by Swanson's, in most supermarkets.

A number of the recipes which follow include soy milk or rice milk. After you have added either of these, be sure to heat or reheat the soup very gently to prevent curdling. If the soup does curdle, puree it in a blender to make it smooth again.

Commercially prepared soups are usually very high in sodium, and as a result, most people are accustomed to soup which tastes quite salty. I have tried to minimize the use of salt while maintaining a flavor that is reasonably familiar to the average palate. In most of the recipes the salt is added last and I have specified that it be "added to taste," which may be more or less than the amount I have suggested.

Lentil Barley Soup

Serves 8

This hearty soup is easy to assemble and cooks in a single pot. It is thick enough to be considered a stew, though you can add more water or stock if you want a thinner soup.

1	**cup lentils, rinsed**
1/2	**cup hulled or pearled barley**
6	**cups water or vegetable stock**
1	**onion, chopped**
2	**garlic cloves, pressed or crushed**
2	**carrots, sliced**
2	**stalks celery, sliced**
1/2	**teaspoon oregano**
1/2	**teaspoon ground cumin**
1/4	**teaspoon black pepper**
1/8-1/4	**teaspoon red pepper flakes**
1/2-1	**teaspoon salt**

Place all the ingredients except salt into a large pot and bring to a simmer. Cover and cook, stirring occasionally, until the lentils are tender, about 1 hour. Add salt to taste.

Per serving: 78 calories; 4 g protein; 16 g carbohydrate; 0 g fat; 150 mg sodium; 0 mg cholesterol

Split Pea Soup

Serves 8

There's nothing quite like split pea soup, simmering on the stove, to make a place feel like home. This simple soup is made in a single pot and contains no added fat.

2	cups split peas
6	cups water
1	medium onion, chopped
2	garlic cloves, pressed or crushed
2	carrots, sliced or diced
2	stalks celery, sliced
1	potato, scrubbed and diced
1/2	teaspoon marjoram
1/2	teaspoon basil
1/4	teaspoon ground cumin
1/4	teaspoon black pepper
1/2-1	teaspoon salt

Rinse the split peas, then place them in a large pot with all the remaining ingredients except salt. Bring to a simmer, then cover loosely and cook until the peas are tender, about 1 hour. Add salt to taste.

Per serving: 189 calories; 10 g protein; 36 g carbohydrate; 0 g fat; 217 mg sodium; 0 mg cholesterol

Simple Golden Broth

Serves 6

This is a soup to cure what ails you! A golden broth that's easy to make and freezes perfectly.

1	onion, chopped
4	garlic cloves, minced
1	cup yellow split peas
1/2	teaspoon turmeric
4	cups water or vegetable stock
1/2-1	teaspoon salt

Place the onion, garlic, split peas, turmeric, and water or vegetable stock into a pot. Bring to a simmer, then cover and cook until the peas are tender, about 50 minutes.

Puree in a blender until smooth. Be sure to start on low speed and hold the lid on tightly. Add salt to taste.

For a thinner broth: Puree, then strain through a sieve. Add salt to taste.

Per serving: 53 calories; 3 g protein; 10 g carbohydrate; 0 g fat; 357 mg sodium; 0 mg cholesterol

Green Velvet Soup

Serves 10

This beautiful soup is perfect for children (of any age!) who won't eat vegetables. Behind its innocent split pea appearance lurks an abundance of nutritious green vegetables.

1	onion, chopped
2	stalks celery, sliced
2	potatoes, scrubbed and diced
3/4	cup split peas, rinsed
2	bay leaves
6	cups water or vegetable stock
2	medium zucchini, diced
1	medium stalk broccoli, chopped
4	cups spinach, chopped
1/2	teaspoon basil
1/4	teaspoon black pepper
1	teaspoon salt

Place the onion, celery, potatoes, split peas, and bay leaves in a large pot with the water or stock and bring to a boil. Lower heat, cover, and simmer 1 hour.

Remove the bay leaves. Add the zucchini, broccoli, spinach, basil, and black pepper. Simmer 20 minutes.

Transfer to a blender in several small batches and puree until completely smooth, holding the lid on tightly. Return to the pot, add salt to taste, and heat until steamy.

Per serving: 120 calories; 5 g protein; 24 g carbohydrate; 0 g fat; 238 mg sodium; 0 mg cholesterol

Chili Potato Soup

Serves 8

This is a spicy alternative to traditional potato soup. Look for canned, diced chilies in your supermarket ("Ortega" is a widely available brand).

4	large russet potatoes, peeled and diced
3	cups water
1	tablespoon olive oil
1	large onion, chopped
2	garlic cloves, crushed or minced
1	large red or green bell pepper, diced
1	teaspoon cumin
1	teaspoon basil
1/4	teaspoon black pepper
1	4-ounce can diced chilies
2	cups soy milk
1 1/4	teaspoons salt
2	green onions, finely chopped, including tops

Simmer the potatoes in 3 cups of water in a covered pot until tender, about 20 minutes. Mash the potatoes in the cooking water, leaving some chunks, and set aside.

Heat the oil in a large pot and sauté the onion for 5 minutes. Add the garlic, bell pepper, cumin, basil, and black pepper. Cook another 5 minutes.

Add the potatoes with their cooking liquid, the diced chilies, and the soy milk. Stir to blend, then heat gently (do not boil!) until hot and steamy. Add salt to taste, sprinkle with chopped green onions, and serve.

Per serving: 165 calories; 3 g protein; 34 g carbohydrate; 2 g fat; 308 mg sodium; 0 mg cholesterol

Golden Mushroom Soup

Serves 6

I love to serve this soup over toasted French bread. Add a tossed green salad for a perfectly marvelous meal.

2	onions, chopped
1	pound mushrooms, sliced
1	tablespoon paprika
1 1/2	teaspoons dill weed
1	teaspoon caraway seeds (optional)
1/8	teaspoon black pepper
3	tablespoons soy sauce
1	cup water or vegetable stock
1	tablespoon olive oil
2	tablespoons flour
2	cups soy milk or rice milk
2	tablespoons lemon juice
3	tablespoons red wine (optional)

Heat 1/2 cup of water in a large pot and add the onions. Cook over high heat, stirring often, until the onions are soft and all the water has evaporated, about 5 minutes. Add another 1/4 cup of water, stir to loosen any bits of onion that have stuck to the pan, and continue cooking until most of the water has evaporated, about 3 minutes.

Add the sliced mushrooms, paprika, dill weed, caraway seeds, and black pepper. Lower the heat slightly, cover and cook 5 minutes, stirring frequently.

Add the soy sauce and water or stock. Cover and simmer 10 minutes.

In a separate pan, mix the olive oil and flour to form a thick paste. Cook, stirring constantly, for 1 minute, then whisk in the soy milk or rice milk and cook over medium heat, stirring frequently, until steamy and slightly thickened.

Add the milk mixture to the soup. Stir in the lemon juice and red wine just before serving.

Per serving: 105 calories; 4 g protein; 17 g carbohydrate; 1.5 g fat; 337 mg sodium; 0 mg cholesterol

Spicy Pumpkin Soup

Serves 6

This soup, which is somewhat spicy and also slightly sweet has a definite Indian flavor. Although the recipe calls for pumpkin, I've also used pureed winter squash, yams, and even cooked carrots with equally delicious results.

1	tablespoon olive oil
1	onion chopped
2	garlic cloves, minced
1/2	teaspoon mustard seeds
1/2	teaspoon turmeric
1/2	teaspoon ginger
1/2	teaspoon cumin
1/4	teaspoon cinnamon
1/8	teaspoon cayenne
3/4	teaspoon salt
2	cups water or vegetable stock
1	15-ounce can pumpkin
2	tablespoons maple syrup or other sweetener
1	tablespoon lemon juice
2	cups soy milk

fresh cilantro, chopped (optional)

Heat the oil in a large pot then add the onion and garlic and cook over medium heat until the onion is soft, about 5 minutes.

Add the mustard seeds, turmeric, ginger, cumin, cinnamon, cayenne, and salt. Cook over medium heat for 2 minutes, stirring constantly.

Whisk in the water or vegetable stock, pumpkin, maple syrup, and lemon juice. Simmer 15 minutes.

Stir in the soy milk, then puree the soup in a blender in two or three batches until very smooth. Return it to the pan and heat over a medium flame until hot and steamy (do not let it boil), about 10 minutes.

Serve with a sprinkling of fresh cilantro if desired.

Per serving: 106 calories; 2 g protein; 18 g carbohydrate; 3 g fat; 302 mg sodium; 0 mg cholesterol

Tomato Bisque

Serves 8

When I originally developed this soup, I was attempting to emulate my childhood mainstay, Cream of Tomato Soup. Hence the name "Tomato Bisque," describing a smooth cream soup. More recently, I find that I actually prefer a chunkier version, and I have omitted the blending step. I considered rewriting the recipe to reflect this change of heart (or taste), but decided to leave the choice to you: if you want a smooth soup, include the blending step described below. If you prefer chunks, skip that step.

1	**onion, chopped**
3	**stalks celery, sliced, including tops**
1	**28-ounce can crushed tomatoes**
1	**cup water or vegetable stock**
2	**tablespoons apple juice concentrate or 2 1/2 teaspoons sugar**
1/2	**teaspoon paprika**
1/2	**teaspoon basil**
1/4	**teaspoon black pepper**
2	**teaspoons olive oil**
2	**tablespoons flour**
2	**cups soy milk or rice milk**
1/2	**teaspoon salt (optional)**

Combine the onion, celery, crushed tomatoes, water, apple juice concentrate or sugar, paprika, basil, and black pepper in a pot. Cover and simmer for 15 minutes.

For a smooth soup, transfer to a blender in two or three small batches and puree until very smooth, then pour it back into the pot. Skip this step if you prefer a chunky soup.

In a separate pan, combine the oil and flour (it will be very thick). Cook, stirring constantly for 1 minute. Whisk in the soy milk or rice milk and cook over medium heat, stirring frequently until steamy and slightly thickened, then add it to the soup. Add salt to taste.

Per serving: 104 calories; 3 g protein; 18 g carbohydrate; 2 g fat; 265 mg sodium; 0 mg cholesterol

Garbanzo and Cabbage Soup

Serves 6

This soup is surprisingly quick to make. Serve it with crusty French bread and a green salad.

2	teaspoons olive oil
1	onion, chopped
1	garlic clove, crushed
1	cup chopped tomato, fresh or canned
2	cups chopped cabbage
1	potato, diced
1/4	cup finely chopped fresh parsley
4	cups water or vegetable stock
1	15-ounce can garbanzo beans, drained
1	teaspoon paprika
1/4	teaspoon black pepper
1/2-1	teaspoon salt

Heat the oil in a large pot and sauté the onion until it is soft, about 3 minutes.

Add the garlic, chopped tomato, cabbage, potato, parsley, water or stock, garbanzo beans, paprika, and black pepper. Simmer until the potato and cabbage are tender, about 15 minutes.

Ladle approximately 3 cups of the soup into a blender. Blend until smooth, being sure to hold the lid on tightly and start on low speed. Return the blended soup to the pot and stir to mix, adding salt to taste.

Per serving: 141 calories; 4 g protein; 25 g carbohydrate; 2 g fat; 192 mg sodium; 0 mg cholesterol

Minestrone

Serves 8

This is a hearty and delicious vegetable soup which takes kindly to embellishment with additional vegetables if you are so inclined.

2	teaspoons olive oil or 1/2 cup water
1	onion, chopped
2	garlic cloves, minced
3	cups tomato juice
3	cups, water
2	carrots, cut into chunks
1	stalk celery, sliced, including top
2	medium potatoes, scrubbed and cut into chunks
2	tablespoons chopped parsley
1 1/2	teaspoons basil
1/4	teaspoon black pepper
1	medium zucchini, diced
1/2	cup pasta shells
2 1/2	cups chopped greens (spinach, kale, bok choy)
1	15-ounce can kidney beans
1/2-1	teaspoon salt

Heat the oil or water in a large pot and add the onion and garlic. Cook over medium high heat until the onion is soft, about 5 minutes.

Add the tomato juice, water, carrots, celery, potatoes, parsley, basil, and black pepper. Bring to a simmer, then cover and cook 20 minutes.

Add the zucchini, pasta, chopped greens, and kidney beans with their liquid. Cover and simmer for 20 minutes, until the pasta is tender.

Add salt to taste. Extra tomato juice or water may be added if a thinner soup is desired.

Per serving (with oil):   179 calories; 6 g protein; 35 g carbohydrate; 1 g fat; 356 mg sodium; 0 mg cholesterol

Per serving (without oil):   169 calories; 6 g protein; 35 g carbohydrate; 0 g fat; 356 mg sodium; 0 mg cholesterol

Black Bean Bisque

Serves 8

This is a perfect make-ahead soup because it tastes even better the second day.

1	**cup dry black beans**
6	**cups water or vegetable stock**
2	**bay leaves**
1	**onion, chopped**
2	**teaspoons olive oil or** 1/2 **cup water**
2	**stalks celery, chopped**
1	**large carrot, chopped**
1	**potato, diced**
2	**large garlic cloves, crushed**
1	**teaspoon oregano**
1/4	**teaspoon savory**
1/8	**teaspoon black pepper**
2	**tablespoons lemon juice**
1	**teaspoon salt**

Rinse the beans, then soak them in about 5 cups of water for 6 to 8 hours or overnight. Pour off the soaking water and place the beans in a pot with 6 cups of fresh water or stock and the bay leaves. Simmer until tender, 1 to 1 1/2 hours.

In a large skillet, cook the onion in olive oil or water until soft, about 5 minutes. Add the celery, carrot and potato and cook an additional 3 minutes, stirring constantly. Add the vegetables to the cooked beans, along with the garlic, oregano, savory, and black pepper. Simmer 1 hour.

Remove the bay leaves. Puree the soup in small batches in a blender until very smooth. Be sure to start on low speed and hold the lid held on tightly. Pour the soup back into the pan and stir in the lemon juice and salt. Heat until steamy.

Crockpot Version: Clean and soak beans as above. Place all the ingredients except the oil, lemon juice and salt into a crockpot. Cover and cook on high until the beans are tender, about 3 hours if you start with boiling water, 6 to 8 hours if you start with cold water. Remove the bay leaves. Puree the soup in small batches in a blender until very smooth, starting on low speed and holding the lid on tightly. Return to a large pot and add the lemon juice and salt. Heat until the soup is steamy.

Per serving (with oil):   149 calories; 5 g protein; 28 g carbohydrate; 2 g fat; 376 mg sodium
        0 mg cholesterol

Per serving (without oil): 136 calories; 5 g protein; 28 g carbohydrate; 0.3 g fat; 376 mg sodium
        0 mg cholesterol

Navy Bean Soup

Serves 8

Serve this hearty soup with Braised Cabbage and Quick and Easy Brown Bread.

1	cup dry navy beans (or other small white beans)
6	cups water

1	onion, chopped
2	garlic cloves, pressed or crushed
1	large carrot, sliced
3	stalks celery, sliced
1	large potato, scrubbed and diced
1	large yam, peeled and diced
2	bay leaves

1/4	cup chopped fresh parsley
1/4	teaspoon thyme
1/4	teaspoon black pepper
1/4	teaspoon liquid smoke (optional)
1-1 1/2	teaspoons salt

Rinse the beans, then soak them for 6 to 8 hours in about 4 cups of water.

Pour off the soak water and place the beans in a pot with 6 cups of fresh water. Add the onion, garlic, carrot, celery, potato, yam, and bay leaves. Bring to a simmer and cook, loosely covered, until the beans are tender, about 1 hour.

When the beans are tender, transfer about 3 cups of the soup to a blender. Add the parsley, thyme, black pepper, and liquid smoke if you are using it. Blend until completely smooth, being sure to start on low speed and hold the lid on tightly. Transfer to a bowl and repeat the blending process until all the soup is blended (or leave some of it unblended if you choose). Return the soup to the pot, add salt to taste, and heat until steamy.

Per serving: 97 calories; 3 g protein; 21 g carbohydrate; 0 g fat; 288 mg sodium; 0 mg cholesterol

Cuban Black Bean Soup

Serves 6 to 8

This savory black bean soup is served with marinated brown rice. What makes it really special is to top it with a crisp green salad, a fat-free vinaigrette, and salsa.

1	**cup dry black beans**
6	**cups water or vegetable stock**
2	**teaspoons olive oil**
1	**onion, chopped**
1	**bell pepper, diced**
5	**garlic cloves, minced**
1 1/2	**teaspoons cumin**
1 1/2	**teaspoons oregano**
2	**tablespoons cider vinegar**
1	**teaspoon salt**

Rinse the beans, then soak them in about 5 cups of water for 6 to 8 hours or overnight. Pour off the soaking water and place the beans in a pot with 6 cups of fresh water or vegetable stock. Simmer until tender, 1 to 1 1/2 hours.

While the beans cook, prepare the rice marinade (recipe follows).

When the beans are tender heat the oil in a large skillet and sauté the onion, bell pepper, garlic, cumin, and oregano for 6 minutes, stirring frequently. Add a tablespoon or two of water if the mixture begins to stick. Add to the beans, then cover and simmer 25 minutes. Stir in the cider vinegar and salt.

To serve, spoon the soup into individual bowls and top it with about 1/2 cup of the marinated rice.

Marinated Rice:

2	**cups cooked brown rice (see page 96)**
1/2	**cup finely chopped onion**
1	**garlic clove, pressed or crushed**
1/4	**cup cider vinegar**
1	**tablespoon olive oil**

Combine the cooked rice with the onion, garlic, vinegar, and olive oil. Stir to mix, then cover and let stand about 1 hour.

Per serving: 174 calories; 5 g protein; 31 g carbohydrate; 3 g fat; 294 mg sodium; 0 mg cholesterol

Simply Wonderful Vegetable Stew

Serves 8

This delicious stew is made with relatively few ingredients and is quick to prepare. Serve it with a fresh green salad and crusty sourdough French bread.

2	**teaspoons olive oil or** 1/2 **cup water**
2	**medium onions, chopped**
1	**28-ounce can crushed tomatoes**
2	**garlic cloves, crushed or pressed**
1	**large green bell pepper, diced**
6	**medium red potatoes, unpeeled, cut into** 1/2-**inch chunks**
1	**teaspoon basil**
1	**teaspoon oregano**
1	**teaspoon Fines Herbes or mixed Italian herbs**
1	**cup water or vegetable stock**
1/4-1/2	**teaspoon salt**
1 - 2	**cups green peas, fresh or frozen**

Heat the oil or water in a large pot and cook the onions until soft, about 5 minutes.

Add the tomatoes, garlic, bell pepper, potatoes, herbs, and 1 cup of water or stock. Bring to a simmer, then cover and cook, stirring occasionally, until the potatoes are just tender, 20 to 25 minutes. If the stew begins to stick, add another cup of water.

Add salt to taste, then stir in the peas. Continue cooking until heated through.

Per serving (with oil):   179 calories; 4 g protein; 37 g carbohydrate; 1.3 g fat; 255 mg sodium;
               0 mg cholesterol

Per serving (without oil):   169 calories; 4 g protein; 37 g carbohydrate; 0 g fat; 255 mg sodium;
               0 mg cholesterol

Winter Squash and Hominy Stew

Serves 8

There are many varieties of winter squash, each with its characteristic appearance and flavor. Any variety will work well in this stew—my favorites are butternut, kabocha, and delicata. Hominy is corn which has been treated with lime, giving it an unusual nutty flavor and increased nutritional value. It is available in most supermarkets with the canned vegetables. Serve this stew with warm tortillas or cornbread and a crisp green salad.

1	pound winter squash (butternut, kabocha, etc.)
1	tablespoon olive oil
1	onion, chopped
1	bell pepper, diced
3	large garlic cloves, minced
2	teaspoons oregano
1	teaspoon cumin
1	tablespoon flour
1	tablespoon chili powder
1	15-ounce can crushed tomatoes
1	29-ounce can hominy, drained
3 1/2	cups water or vegetable stock
1/2	teaspoon salt
1-2	tablespoons chopped cilantro

Cut the squash in half and scoop out the seeds with a spoon. Peel the squash (see note below), then cut it into 1/2-inch cubes and set aside.

Heat the olive oil in a large pot and sauté the onion for 3 minutes. Add the bell pepper, garlic, oregano, and cumin. Cook 3 minutes. Stir in the flour and chili powder and cook 30 seconds longer, stirring constantly.

Add the squash, tomatoes, hominy, and water or vegetable stock. Bring to a simmer and cook, uncovered, until the squash is completely tender, about 25 minutes. Add salt to taste. Garnish with chopped fresh cilantro if desired.

Note: You can use a potato peeler to peel some varieties like butternut. Others, like the kabocha, have tougher skins and must be peeled with a knife. One way to make any squash easier to peel is to heat it in a microwave until it is just slightly softened, about 5 minutes.

Per serving: 128 calories; 3 g protein; 22 g carbohydrate; 3 g fat; 141 mg sodium; 0 mg cholesterol

Vegetable Stock

Makes about 8 cups

Use this stock to enhance the flavor of soups and stews, or use it as the liquid for cooking rice and other grains. For a darker stock, caramelize the onions by sautéing them in 1 tablespoon of olive oil over medium heat, stirring frequently, until they are dark brown. This will take 15 to 20 minutes.

Look for dried shitake mushrooms in natural food stores, ethnic markets, or in the imported food section of your supermarket.

1	**ounce dried shitake mushrooms**
1	**cup hot water**
1	**onion, chopped**
2	**carrots, scrubbed and diced**
2	**stalks celery, sliced**
1/4	**pound fresh mushrooms, sliced**
1	**leek, coarsely chopped**
2	**garlic cloves, crushed**
2	**bay leaves**
1/4	**teaspoon thyme**
1/8	**teaspoon sage**
1	**teaspoon salt**
9	**cups water**

Place the shitake mushrooms in a small bowl and cover them with hot water. Set aside until soft, 20 to 30 minutes.

Place the onions, carrots, celery, mushrooms, leek, and garlic into a large pot with the bay leaves, thyme, sage, salt, and water. When the shitake mushrooms are soft, pour off and reserve the soaking liquid. Rinse the mushrooms to remove any grit then add them to the pot. Strain the soaking water and add it to the pot. Cover the pot and bring it to a boil, then reduce the heat and simmer 45 minutes. Strain the stock through a fine-meshed sieve.

Per cup: 39 calories; 1 g protein; 8 g carbohydrate; 0 g fat; 284 mg sodium; 0 mg cholesterol

VEGETABLES

Until he extends the circle of his compassion to all living things,
man will not himself find peace.
Albert Schweitzer

Broccoli with Mustard Vinaigrette

6 servings

For years I tried to find a way to get my parents to eat broccoli. I talked about its tremendous nutritional benefits, I hid it in soups, added it to salads and casseroles, and tossed it with pasta . . . all to no avail. One day I tried this recipe, and broccoli is now a regular addition to their meals. Ah, the sweet taste of success!

1	**bunch broccoli (3 to 4 stalks)**
1/4	**cup seasoned rice vinegar**
1	**teaspoon stone ground or Dijon mustard**
1	**garlic clove, crushed**

Break the broccoli into bite-sized florets. Peel the stems and slice them into 1/4-inch thick rounds. Steam until just tender, about 5 minutes.

While the broccoli is steaming, whisk the vinegar, mustard, and garlic together in a serving bowl. Add the steamed broccoli and toss to mix. Serve immediately.

Per serving: 62 calories; 2.5 g protein; 12 g carbohydrate; 0 g fat; 39 mg sodium; 0 mg cholesterol

Broccoli with Sun-dried Tomatoes

Serves 6

You'll love the tangy flavor of sun-dried tomatoes with steamed broccoli.

1	**bunch broccoli**
6	**sun-dried tomatoes in olive oil**

Break or cut the broccoli into florets; peel and slice the stems into rounds. Steam over boiling water until just tender, about 5 minutes.

While the broccoli is cooking, remove the sun-dried tomatoes from the olive oil and cut them into small pieces. Place them in a serving dish, and add the broccoli when it is tender. Toss and serve.

Per serving: 29 calories; 1 g protein; 4 g carbohydrate; 1 g fat; 9 mg sodium; 0 mg cholesterol

Collards & Kale

Serves 2 to 4

Collard greens and kale are excellent sources of calcium as well as rich sources of beta carotene. The simplest way to prepare them is to remove the tough stems and steam the chopped leaves like spinach. They can also be added to soups and stews. I especially enjoy them when they are prepared in the following manner with soy sauce and garlic.

1	**bunch collard greens or kale (6 to 8 cups chopped)**
1/2	**cup water**
2	**teaspoons soy sauce**
2-3	**garlic cloves, minced**

Wash the greens, remove the stems, and chop the leaves into 1/2-inch wide strips.

Heat the water and soy sauce in a large pot or skillet. Add the garlic and cook it 1 to 2 minutes. Add the chopped greens and toss to mix. Cover and cook over medium heat until tender, about 5 minutes.

Per 1 cup: 61 calories; 3 g protein; 11 g carbohydrate; 0 g fat; 101 mg sodium; 0 mg cholesterol

Braised Cabbage

Serves 4

I had never eaten cooked cabbage until my husband's mother, Adrien Avis, introduced me to the simple pleasures of this delicious vegetable. Try this recipe and you'll see what I mean.

1/2	**cup water**
2	**cups cabbage, coarsely chopped**
1/2	**teaspoon caraway seeds (optional)**
salt and fresh ground black pepper	

Bring the water to a boil in a skillet or saucepan and add the cabbage and caraway seeds if desired. Cover and cook until just tender, about 5 minutes. Sprinkle with salt and black pepper.

Per serving: 16 calories; 0.5 g protein; 4 g carbohydrate; 0 g fat; 13 mg sodium; 0 mg cholesterol

Italian Green Beans

Serves 6 to 8

11/2   **pounds fresh green beans**

1   **tablespoon olive oil**
2   **cups chopped tomatoes, fresh or canned**
2   **large garlic cloves, minced**
2   **tablespoons chopped fresh basil or 1 teaspoon dried basil**
salt and fresh ground pepper to taste

Trim the beans and cut or break them into bite-sized lengths. Steam until just tender, about 10 minutes, then set aside.

Heat the oil in a large skillet, then add the tomatoes and garlic. Simmer gently for 10 minutes. Add the green beans and basil and cook 5 minutes longer, stirring occasionally. Add salt and pepper to taste.

Per serving: 72 calories; 2 g protein; 11 g carbohydrate; 2 g fat; 122 mg sodium; 0 mg cholesterol

Green Beans with Toasted Almonds

Serves 6

Sesame oil, seasoned rice vinegar, and soy sauce give these green beans an Asian flair.

1   **pound fresh green beans**

2   **teaspoons toasted sesame oil**
1   **onion, chopped**
1/4   **cup slivered almonds**
1   **tablespoon seasoned rice vinegar**
1   **tablespoon soy sauce**

Trim the beans and break them into bite-sized pieces. Steam until tender, about 10 minutes. Set aside.

Heat the oil in a large skillet and sauté the onion and almonds until the onion is soft, about 3 minutes. Lower the heat and add the vinegar. Continue cooking, stirring often, until the onions and almonds begin to brown, about 10 minutes. Stir in the soy sauce and cooked green beans. Cook 2 to 3 minutes longer.

Per serving: 77 calories; 2 g protein; 9 g carbohydrate; 3 g fat; 105 mg sodium; 0 mg cholesterol

Beets with Mustard Dressing

Serves 4

Even confirmed beet-haters have been known to enjoy them when they're prepared with this delicious dressing. Serve them as a hot vegetable, or chill them for a salad.

4	**medium beets**
1	**tablespoon stone ground or Dijon mustard**
2	**tablespoons lemon juice**
1	**tablespoon cider vinegar**
1	**teaspoon sugar or other sweetener**
1	**teaspoon dried dill or 1 tablespoon fresh dill**

Wash the beets and cut off the tops (save these to steam for another meal).

Peel the beets, slice them into 1/4-inch thick rounds, and steam over boiling water until tender, about 20 minutes. Remove from heat and place into a serving dish.

Combine the mustard, lemon juice, vinegar, sugar, and dill. Pour over the cooked beets and toss to mix.

Per serving: 31 calories; 1 g protein; 6 g carbohydrate; 0 g fat; 115 mg sodium; 0 mg cholesterol

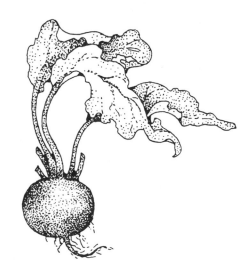

Red Potatoes with Kale

Serves 8

This dish is colorful and delicious. Be sure to use a non-stick skillet.

4	**red potatoes**
1	**bunch kale**
1	**teaspoon toasted sesame oil**
1	**onion, thinly sliced**
2	**garlic cloves, minced**
1/2	**teaspoon black pepper**
1/2	**teaspoon paprika**
5	**teaspoons soy sauce**
2	**tablespoons water**

Scrub the potatoes and cut them into 1/2-inch cubes. Steam over boiling water until just tender when pierced with a fork. Rinse with cold water then drain and set aside.

Rinse the kale and remove the stems. Cut or tear the leaves into small pieces.

Heat the oil in a large non-stick skillet. Add the onion and garlic and sauté 5 minutes.

Add the cooked potatoes, pepper, and paprika. Continue cooking until the potatoes begin to brown, about 5 minutes. Use a spatula to turn the mixture gently as it cooks.

Spread the kale leaves over the top of the potato mixture. Sprinkle with the soy sauce and 2 tablespoons of water. Cover and cook, turning occasionally, until the kale is tender, about 7 minutes.

Per serving: 104 calories; 4 g protein; 20 g carbohydrate; 1 g fat; 164 mg sodium; 0 mg cholesterol

Mashed Potatoes and Gravy

Serves 8

American Traditional at its finest! Serve with Neat Loaf for a meal that will satisfy even the most committed carnivore!

4	**large russet potatoes, peeled and diced**
2	**cups water**
1/2-1	**teaspoon salt**
1/2-1	**cup soy milk or rice milk**
2	**teaspoons olive or toasted sesame oil**
1	**small onion, chopped (about 1/2 cup)**
1	**cup thinly sliced mushrooms**
2	**tablespoons flour**
1	**tablespoon soy sauce**
1/4	**teaspoon black pepper**

Place the potatoes in a pot with 2 cups of water and 1/2 teaspoon salt. Simmer until tender, about 15 to 20 minutes. Drain and reserve the liquid. Mash the potatoes, then add enough soy milk or rice milk to make the potatoes creamy. Add salt to taste. Cover and set aside.

Heat the oil in a large skillet and sauté the onion and mushrooms over high heat, stirring frequently, until they are browned, about 5 minutes.

Whisk the flour into the potato cooking liquid along with the soy sauce and black pepper. Add to the onion-mushroom mixture and cook over medium heat, stirring constantly until thickened.

Note: If you prefer smooth gravy, puree it in a blender. Be sure to start on low speed and hold the lid on tightly.

Per serving: 139 calories; 2.5 g protein; 29 g carbohydrate; 1 g fat; 232 mg sodium; 0 mg cholesterol

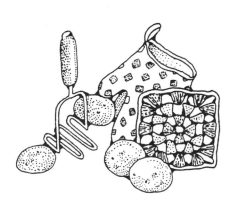

Oven Fries

Serves 4

2	large russet potatoes (about 1 pound)
2	teaspoons olive oil
1	teaspoon paprika
1/4-1/2	teaspoon salt

Preheat the oven to 450°F. For easy cleanup, line a 9 x 13-inch (or larger) baking dish with baking parchment.

Scrub the potatoes, but do not peel. Cut into long, thin strips. Place in a large bowl and toss with the oil, paprika, and salt. Spread in a single layer in the baking dish and bake until tender when pierced with a fork, about 30 minutes.

Per serving: 130 calories; 2 g protein; 26 g carbohydrate; 2 g fat; 141 mg sodium; 0 mg cholesterol

Yams with Cranberries and Apples

Serves 8

This dish is a beautiful blend of sweet and tart flavors which can be enjoyed any time of year. Buy and freeze extra cranberries when they are available in the fall or use dried cranberries.

3	yams, peeled
1	large, tart green apple, peeled and diced
1	tablespoon lemon juice
1/2	cup raw cranberries or 1/3 cup dried cranberries
1/4	cup raisins
1/4	cup orange juice concentrate
2	tablespoons maple syrup
1	tablespoon soy sauce

Preheat the oven to 350°F. Cut the yams into 1-inch chunks and spread in a large baking dish. Toss the apple with the lemon juice and add it to the yams. Sprinkle with cranberries and raisins. Mix the orange juice concentrate, maple syrup, and soy sauce with 1/4 cup water. Pour over the top. Cover and bake until the yams are tender when pierced with a fork, about 1 hour.

Per serving: 138 calories; 2 g protein; 32 g carbohydrate; 0 g fat; 83 mg sodium; 0 mg cholesterol

Winter Squash with Peanut Sauce

Serves 6

Most markets sell a wide variety of delicious winter squashes, with marvelous names like "Delicata," "Butternut," "Kabocha," and "Sweet Dumpling." Each has its characteristic flavor, and all are excellent sources of the anti-oxidant nutrient beta carotene. There are a number of ways to cook winter squash, including baking, microwaving, and steaming it. My preference is to steam it because it is quick and the squash stays moist. If you've never tried dressing winter squash up with peanut sauce, I heartily recommend the following recipe. Enjoy!

1	**large or 3 small winter squash**
1/4	**cup peanut butter**
1/4	**cup hot water**
2	**teaspoons soy sauce**
2	**teaspoons seasoned rice vinegar**
1	**teaspoon sugar or other sweetener**
2	**cloves garlic, minced**
1	**teaspoon fresh ginger, minced or 1/4 teaspoon ginger powder**
1/8	**teaspoon cayenne**

Slice the squash in half and scoop out the seeds. Place it on a vegetable steamer and steam in a covered pot over boiling water until tender when pierced with a fork. The time this takes depends on the variety and size of the squash. Begin checking after 15 minutes. You can also cook the squash in a microwave oven. Follow the manufacturer's instructions.

While the squash cooks, combine the peanut butter, water, soy sauce, seasoned rice vinegar, sugar, garlic, ginger, and cayenne in a small saucepan. Mix with a fork or whisk, then heat gently until the sauce is smooth and slightly thickened. Add more water if the sauce becomes too thick.

When the squash is tender, drizzle it with peanut sauce and serve.

Per serving: 144 calories; 4 g protein; 21 g carbohydrate; 5 g fat; 76 mg sodium; 0 mg cholesterol

Roasted Red Peppers

Roasted red peppers make delicious additions to salads, sauces and soups. You can purchase roasted peppers in jars in most grocery stores, and I often do. However, if you really want that just-roasted flavor, roast the peppers yourself. It's not difficult, and it makes the house smell absolutely wonderful!

one or more large firm red bell peppers

Wash the pepper and place it over an open flame (such as a gas burner on the stove) or under the oven broiler. Turn the pepper with tongs until the skin is charred on all sides. Place it into a bowl and cover the bowl with a plate. Let stand 15 minutes, then remove the charred skin. Cut the pepper in half, saving any juice which drains out, and remove the seeds.

Per pepper: 18 calories; 0.5 g protein; 4 g carbohydrate; 0 g fat; 2 mg sodium; 0 mg cholesterol

Roasted Garlic

Roasted garlic makes a delicious appetizer, or accompaniment to a meal. I place several heads on the table and let people pick off cloves, peel them, and discover the mild taste and creamy texture. Roasted garlic can also be used as a spread on bread, or in salads and dressings. Store it in a sealed container in the refrigerator for up to 2 weeks.

whole garlic bulbs

Select bulbs of garlic which have nice large cloves. Place the entire bulb into a small baking dish and bake in a toaster oven or regular oven at 375°F until the cloves feel soft when pressed, about 30 minutes.

Per bulb: 40 calories; 0 g protein; 10 g carbohydrate; 0 g fat; 10 mg sodium; 0 mg cholesterol

GRAINS
&
SIDE DISHES

*Until he extends the circle of his compassion to all living things,
man will not himself find peace.*
Albert Schweitzer

Brown Rice

Makes 3 cups of cooked rice

For perfect, fluffy brown rice every time, try cooking it with extra water. This technique can be used with short or long grain brown rice, and actually reduces the cooking time: I find that the rice is tender in 35 to 40 minutes. The extra liquid which is poured off makes a marvelous broth for soups or stews.

4-5	**cups water**
1	**cup brown rice (short grain or long grain)**
1/2	**teaspoon salt**

Bring the water to a boil in a saucepan. Rinse and drain the rice then add it to the boiling water along with the salt. Adjust the heat so the rice boils gently, then cover loosely and cook until the rice is soft but still retains a hint of crunchiness, about 35 to 40 minutes. Pour off the excess water. For even fluffier rice, rinse and drain it.

Per 1/2 cup: 115 calories; 2.5 g protein; 25 g carbohydrate; 0 g fat; 176 mg sodium; 0 mg cholesterol

Quick Confetti Rice

Makes about 3 cups

This colorful rice pilaf is made with no added fat, so be sure to use a nonstick skillet.

2	**tablespoons water or vegetable stock**
2	**cups cooked brown rice**
1/2	**cup frozen corn**
1/2	**cup frozen peas**
1/2	**red bell pepper, diced**
1/2	**teaspoon curry powder**
1/4	**cup raisins (optional)**
	salt to taste

Heat the water or vegetable stock in a large nonstick skillet. Add the cooked rice, then use a spatula or the back of a wooden spoon to separate the kernels. Add the corn, peas, bell pepper, curry powder, and raisins. Heat thoroughly. Add salt to taste (you may not need to add salt if the rice was cooked in salted water).

Per 1/2 cup: 109 calories; 2.5 g protein; 24 g carbohydrate; 0 g fat; 112 mg sodium; 0 mg cholesterol

Pilau

Serves 6 to 8

Pilau is the Indian counterpart to the dish we call "pilaf." The seasonings are generally mild, almost sweet, to offset the strong, hot flavors of the curries. Although white rice is used in traditional Indian cooking, brown rice works nicely if you allow additional cooking time. Basmati rice is available in most supermarkets and natural food stores.

2	teaspoons olive or peanut oil
1	cup basmati rice (white or brown)
1/2	teaspoon turmeric
1/4	teaspoon cinnamon
1/8	teaspoon cardamom
1/2	teaspoon salt
1/4	cup slivered almonds
1/4	cup raisins
2	cups boiling water
1/2	cup green peas, fresh or frozen

Heat the oil in a large pot and sauté the rice over medium heat for 3 minutes. Add the turmeric, cinnamon, cardamom, salt, and slivered almonds. Cook for 2 minutes, stirring constantly.

Stir in the raisins, then add the boiling water. Lower the heat to a simmer, cover the pot, and cook until the rice is tender and all the water is absorbed (20 minutes for white rice, 60 minutes for brown rice).

Stir in the peas just before serving (a few minutes sooner if you're using fresh peas).

Per serving: 108 calories; 2 g protein; 19 g carbohydrate; 2 g fat; 150 mg sodium; 0 mg cholesterol

Basmati and Wild Rice Pilaf

Serves 8

*Basmati and wild rice contribute flavor and texture to this delicious, low-fat pilaf.
The nuts can be left out if you want it truly fat-free, though I must admit they add
marvelous flavor and texture to the dish.*

1/4	**cup wild rice, rinsed**
1	**15-ounce can Swanson's Vegetable Broth**
1/2	**cup water**
3/4	**cup brown basmati rice, rinsed**
1	**onion, finely chopped**
2	**garlic cloves, minced**
2	**cups thinly sliced mushrooms**
2	**stalks celery, thinly sliced**
1/2	**teaspoon thyme**
1/2	**teaspoon marjoram**
1/4	**teaspoon black pepper**
1/4	**teaspoons salt**
1/3	**cup finely chopped parsley**
1/3	**cup toasted pecans, chopped (optional)**

Place the wild rice in a saucepan with the vegetable broth and 1/2 cup of water. Stir
to mix, then cover and simmer for 20 minutes. Add the basmati rice, then cover and
continue cooking over very low heat until the rice is tender, about 50 more minutes.

Heat 1/2 cup of water in a large (preferably nonstick) skillet and cook the onion and
garlic until all the water has evaporated and pieces of onion begin to stick to the pan.
Add another 1/4 cup of water, stirring to remove any browned bits of onion, and cook
until the water has evaporated. Repeat this process of adding water and cooking until
it evaporates until the onions are nicely browned, about 15 or 20 minutes.

Lower the heat slightly and add the mushrooms, celery, thyme, marjoram, black
pepper, and salt to the browned onions. Cook, stirring frequently, for 5 minutes. Add
the cooked rice, the parsley, and the chopped pecans. Cook over low heat, turning
gently, until the mixture is very hot.

Per serving (with nuts): 124 calories; 2 g protein; 21 g carbohydrate; 3 g fat; 213 mg sodium;
0 mg cholesterol

Per serving (without nuts): 93 calories; 2 g protein; 20 g carbohydrate; 0 g fat; 213 mg sodium;
0 mg cholesterol

Turkey's Favorite Bread Dressing

Serves 8

Dressing was the only part of the Thanksgiving meal that I really missed when I became a vegetarian. What a happy day when I discovered that it could be made without the turkey!

1	tablespoon olive oil
1	onion, chopped
3	cups sliced mushrooms (about 1/2 pound)
2	celery stalks, sliced
4	cups cubed bread
1/3	cup finely chopped parsley
1/2	teaspoon thyme
1/2	teaspoon marjoram
1/2	teaspoon sage
1/8	teaspoon black pepper
1/2	teaspoon salt
1	cup (approximately) very hot water or vegetable stock

Heat the oil in a large pot or skillet and sauté the onion for 5 minutes.

Add the sliced mushrooms and celery and cook over medium heat until the mushrooms begin to brown, about 5 minutes.

Preheat the oven to 350°F. Stir in the bread, parsley, thyme, marjoram, sage, black pepper, and salt. Lower the heat and continue cooking for 3 minutes, then stir in the water or stock a little at a time until the dressing obtains desired moistness. Spread in an oil-sprayed baking dish, cover and bake for 20 minutes. Remove cover and bake 10 minutes longer.

Per serving: 91 calories; 3 g protein; 14 g carbohydrate; 2 g fat; 297 mg sodium; 0 mg cholesterol

Bulgur

Makes 2 1/2 cups

Bulgur is a delicious easily-prepared grain. It is made from whole wheat kernels which have been cracked and toasted, giving it a wonderful, nutty flavor. Serve it plain, or use it in pilafs and salads.

1	**cup uncooked bulgur**
1/2	**teaspoon salt**
2	**cups boiling water**

Mix the bulgur and salt in a large bowl then pour the boiling water over it. Cover and let stand until tender, about 25 minutes.

Alternate cooking method: Bring the water to a boil then add the salt and bulgur. Reduce heat to a simmer, then cover and cook until the bulgur is tender, about 15 minutes.

Per 1/2 cup: 112 calories; 4 g protein; 24 g carbohydrate; 0 g fat; 213 mg sodium; 0 mg cholesterol

Spicy Bulgur Pilaf

Makes about 3 cups

Serve this Mexican pilaf with chili or refried beans and a green salad.

1	**medium onion, chopped**
2	**teaspoons olive oil**
2	**garlic cloves, minced**
1	**cup uncooked bulgur**
2	**teaspoons chili powder**
1	**teaspoon ground cumin**
1/8	**teaspoon celery seeds**
1/2	**red bell pepper, finely diced**
1/2	**teaspoon salt**
1 3/4	**cups boiling water or vegetable stock**

Sauté the onion in olive oil in a large skillet for 5 minutes. Stir in the garlic, bulgur, chili powder, cumin, and celery seeds. Continue cooking 3 minutes, stirring frequently. Add the bell pepper and salt, then pour in the boiling water or vegetable stock. Cover tightly and let stand until all the liquid is absorbed, about 20 minutes.

Per 1/2 cup: 144 calories; 5 g protein; 27 g carbohydrate; 2 g fat; 186 mg sodium; 0 mg cholesterol

Chinese Bulgur

Makes about 3 cups

This quick side dish is perfect with any vegetable stir-fry.

1	**cup uncooked bulgur**
1/2	**teaspoon salt**
13/4	**cups boiling water**
2	**teaspoons toasted sesame oil**
1	**teaspoon fresh minced ginger**
1	**garlic clove, minced**
1/2	**cup finely sliced green onions, including tops**
1/2	**cup sliced water chestnuts**
11/2	**tablespoons soy sauce**
1/8	**teaspoon black pepper**

Place the bulgur and salt in a bowl, then add the boiling water. Cover and let stand until all the water is absorbed, about 25 minutes.

Heat the toasted sesame oil in a large nonstick skillet, then add the ginger, garlic, and green onions. Cook 1 minute. Stir in the water chestnuts, soaked bulgur, soy sauce, and black pepper. Cook, turning gently with a spatula until hot, about 3 minutes.

Per 1/2 cup: 145 calories; 5 g protein; 27 g carbohydrate; 2 g fat; 331 mg sodium; 0 mg cholesterol

Polenta

Makes 4 cups

Polenta, a staple grain in northern Italy, is delicious with marinara or any other spicy vegetable sauce. It is prepared much like a hot breakfast cereal and has a consistency similar to Cream of Wheat. For a firmer version, pour the hot polenta into a bread pan and chill it completely. It will become a solid loaf from which slices can be cut, then fried, broiled, or grilled.

1	**cup polenta**
4	**cups water**
1/2	**teaspoon salt**
1	**teaspoon crushed rosemary (optional)**

Mix the polenta with the water and salt in a large pot. Add the rosemary if desired. Bring to a simmer, and cook, stirring frequently until very thick, about 15 minutes.

Per 1/2 cup: 62 calories; 1.5 g protein; 14 g carbohydrate; 0 g fat; 267 mg sodium; 0 mg cholesterol

Couscous

Makes about 3 cups

Couscous is actually a very small pasta made from wheat. Serve it plain, as a pilaf or salad, or topped with vegetables and sauce. Most supermarkets sell couscous, and natural food stores often sell the whole wheat variety.

11/2	**cups boiling water**
1	**cup couscous**
1/2	**teaspoon salt**

Bring the water to a boil in a small pan, then stir in the couscous and salt. Remove the pan from the heat, cover and let stand 10 to 15 minutes. Fluff the couscous with a fork before serving.

Per 1/2 cup: 91 calories; 3 g protein; 20 g carbohydrate; 0 g fat; 182 mg sodium; 0 mg cholesterol

Fettucine with Roasted Red Pepper Sauce

Serves 6

Roasted red peppers and garlic make a delicious pasta sauce. You can roast the peppers yourself (see page 94), or purchase jars of roasted peppers in most supermarkets.

1	**tablespoon pine nuts**
3	**roasted red peppers**
1	**garlic clove, crushed**
1 1/2	**tablespoons Balsamic vinegar**
1	**tablespoon olive oil**
1/4	**teaspoon salt**
8	**ounces fettucine**

Toast the pinenuts in a 350°F oven or toaster oven for 8 to 10 minutes.

Combine the roasted peppers, garlic, pinenuts, vinegar, oil, and salt in a blender or food processor and puree until smooth.

Cook the pasta in boiling water until it is tender. Drain and rinse, then toss with the sauce. Serve immediately.

Per serving: 97 calories; 3 g protein; 14 g carbohydrate; 3 g fat; 91 mg sodium; 0 mg cholesterol

Pasta with Peanut Sauce

Serves 8

Peanut sauce takes just minutes to prepare and gives pasta a whole new personality. Serve this dish with an assortment of lightly steamed vegetables for a complete and satisfying meal.

8	**ounces uncooked pasta**
1/2	**cup peanut butter**
1	**cup hot water**
2	**tablespoons soy sauce**
2	**tablespoons seasoned rice vinegar**
1	**tablespoon sugar or other sweetener**
2	**garlic cloves, minced**
1/2	**teaspoon ginger powder**
1/4	**teaspoon red pepper flakes or a pinch of cayenne**
3	**green onions including tops, finely chopped**

Cook the pasta in rapidly boiling water until it is just tender. Rinse and drain.

While the pasta is cooking, combine the peanut butter, water, soy sauce, vinegar, sugar, garlic, ginger, and red pepper flakes in a saucepan and whisk until smooth. Heat gently until slightly thickened. Add more water if the sauce becomes too thick.

Toss the cooked pasta with the sauce and sprinkle with chopped green onions. Serve immediately.

Per serving: 147 calories; 5 g protein; 15 g carbohydrate; 7 g fat; 153 mg sodium; 0 mg cholesterol

MAIN DISHES

*Until he extends the circle of his compassion to all living things,
man will not himself find peace.*
Albert Schweitzer

Shepherd's Pie

Serves 8 to 10

This is a hearty and satisfying vegetable stew with a top "crust" of mashed potatoes.

4	**large russet potatoes**
1/2-1	**cup soy milk or rice milk**
1/2	**teaspoon salt**
1/2	**cup water or vegetable stock**
2	**onions, chopped**
1	**large bell pepper, diced**
2	**carrots, sliced**
2	**stalks of celery, sliced**
21/2	**cups sliced mushrooms (about 1/2 pound)**
1	**15-ounce can crushed or ground tomatoes**
1	**15-ounce can kidney beans, drained**
1/2	**teaspoon paprika**
1/2	**teaspoon black pepper**
2	**tablespoons soy sauce**

Scrub and dice the potatoes, then simmer them in 1 cup of water until tender, about 15 minutes. Mash, without draining them, then add enough soy milk or rice milk to make them smooth and spreadable.   Mix in the salt and set aside.

Heat 1/4 cup water or stock in a large pot and add the onions. Cook for 3 minutes then add the bell pepper, carrots, and celery. Cook for 5 minutes over medium heat. Add the mushrooms, then cover the pan and cook an additional 7 minutes, stirring occasionally. Add the tomatoes, kidney beans, paprika, black pepper, and soy sauce. Cover and cook 15 minutes.

Preheat the oven to 350°F. Transfer the vegetables to a 9 x 13-inch baking dish and spread the mashed potatoes evenly over the top. Sprinkle with paprika. Bake for 25 minutes, until hot and bubbly.

Per serving: 217 calories; 6 g protein; 47 g carbohydrate; 0 g fat; 257 mg sodium; 0 mg cholesterol

Pasta with Broccoli and Pine Nuts

Serves 6 to 8

This dish is perfect for a light supper. For a heartier meal, serve it with a bean soup and a crisp green salad.

1	**pound broccoli**
8	**ounces fettuccine**
1	**tablespoon olive oil**
4-8	**large garlic cloves, minced**
1/4	**teaspoon red pepper flakes or a pinch of cayenne**
2	**tablespoons pine nuts**
4	**large tomatoes, diced or 1 28-ounce can chopped tomatoes**
1/4	**teaspoon salt**

Break or cut the broccoli into florets; peel and slice the stems into rounds. Place in a vegetable steamer and set aside.

Cook the pasta in boiling, salted water until it is just tender. Drain and rinse quickly.

While the pasta is cooking, heat the oil in a large skillet and sauté the garlic, red pepper flakes or cayenne, and pine nuts for 1 minute. Add the tomatoes and cook over medium heat for 7 minutes.

While the sauce cooks, steam the broccoli until it is just tender, about 5 minutes. It should be bright green and still slightly crisp. Add it to the tomato sauce.

Spread the pasta on a large platter and top with the sauce. Serve immediately.

Per serving: 150 calories; 5 g protein; 25 g carbohydrate; 3 g fat; 117 mg sodium; 0 mg cholesterol

Pasta Primavera

Serves 8

Vegetable mixture:

1	tablespoon olive oil
1	onion, chopped
2	garlic cloves, minced
2 1/2	cups mushrooms, cleaned and sliced (about 1/2 pound)
1	red bell pepper, diced
2	medium zucchini, diced
1/2	cup chopped fresh parsley
1	teaspoon basil
1/2	teaspoon oregano
1/2	teaspoon thyme
4	large tomatoes, chopped
1/2	teaspoon salt

White sauce:

1 1/2	cups soy milk or rice milk
5	tablespoons flour
3	tablespoons nutritional yeast (optional)
1/2	teaspoon onion powder
1/2	teaspoon salt

8	ounces fettuccine or similar pasta
1/4	cup finely chopped toasted almonds (optional)

Heat the oil in a large pot then add the onion and garlic. Cook until the onion is soft, about 5 minutes. Add the sliced mushrooms, bell pepper, zucchini, and parsley along with the basil, oregano, and thyme. Cook over medium heat for 5 minutes, then stir in the tomatoes. Continue cooking until the bell pepper and zucchini are just tender, 3 to 5 minutes. Add salt to taste.

In a separate pan, whisk the soy milk or rice milk and flour together, then stir in the nutritional yeast, onion powder, and salt. Cook over medium heat, stirring constantly, until thickened. Add to the vegetables and stir to mix.

Cook the pasta in boiling, salted water until it is just tender. Drain and rinse, then combine it with the vegetable mixture, and toss to mix. Sprinkle with toasted almonds if desired. Serve immediately.

Per serving (with nuts): 158 calories; 5 g protein; 24 g carbohydrate; 4 g fat; 294 mg sodium; 0 mg cholesterol

Per serving (without nuts): 130 calories; 4 g protein; 23 g carbohydrate; 2 g fat; 294 mg sodium; 0 mg cholesterol

Pasta with Creamy Tofu

Serves 6

My mother hated to cook (actually, she still does). I remember when Peg Bracken's
I Hate to Cook Book made its appearance in our home and "Tuna Casserole" became a
regular menu item. For some reason, this dish reminds me of that, though of course, it
is made without the tuna.

8	ounces fettuccine
1	tablespoon olive oil
1	onion, chopped
1/2	bell pepper, diced
3	cups sliced mushrooms (about 1/2 pound)
2	garlic cloves, minced
2	tablespoons finely chopped parsley
1/4	teaspoon thyme
1/4	teaspoon black pepper
1/4	cup unbleached flour
1 1/2	cups soy milk or rice milk
1/2	pound firm tofu, crumbled
1	cup green peas, fresh or frozen
1	teaspoon salt

Cook the pasta in boiling, salted water until it is just tender. Drain and rinse, then set
aside.

Heat the olive oil in a large skillet and sauté the onion until it is soft, about 5 minutes.
Add the bell pepper, mushrooms, garlic, chopped parsley, thyme, and black pepper.
Cover and cook until the mushrooms are browned, about 7 minutes.

Whisk the flour and soy milk or rice milk together, and add to mushroom mixture.
Cook until slightly thickened. Stir in the tofu, peas, and salt. Heat thoroughly.

Combine the tofu mixture with the pasta and toss to mix. Serve immediately.

Per serving: 168 calories; 8 g protein; 27 g carbohydrate; 3 g fat; 288 mg sodium; 0 mg cholesterol

Hungarian Goulash

Serves 6 to 8

This hearty goulash is made with seitan ("say-tan"), a high protein wheat product with a meaty taste and texture. It also contains miso, a salty, fermented soyfood, which is added as a flavoring. Miso comes in light and dark varieties. The light versions have a milder flavor, the dark are more robust. Both of these products are sold in natural food stores and Asian markets.

1	**tablespoon toasted sesame oil**
1	**large onion, thinly sliced**
3	**cups sliced mushrooms**
1	**green bell pepper, diced**
1	**red bell pepper, diced**
3	**tablespoons light miso**
1 1/2	**cups water**
1	**28-ounce can crushed tomatoes**
3/4	**cup sauerkraut**
8	**ounces seitan, cut into bite-sized pieces**
4	**teaspoons paprika**
1/2	**teaspoon basil**
1/4	**teaspoon black pepper**
8	**ounces pasta (try tomato-basil fettuccine or red pepper pasta)**

Heat the oil in a large pot or skillet and sauté the onion until it is soft and just beginning to brown, about 5 minutes. Add the sliced mushrooms and bell peppers. Lower the heat slightly, then cover and cook for 8 to 10 minutes, stirring occasionally.

Combine the miso and water, stirring until smooth. Add it to the vegetable mixture, along with the tomatoes, sauerkraut, seitan, paprika, basil, and black pepper. Cover and simmer 10 minutes.

While the goulash simmers, cook the pasta in boiling water according to package directions. Drain, then rinse with hot water, and spread it on a platter. Top with goulash and serve immediately.

Per serving: 195 calories; 20 g protein; 23 g carbohydrate; 2 g fat; 369 mg sodium; 0 mg cholesterol

Stuffed Spaghetti Squash

Serves 8

Spaghetti squash has a crisp texture and rich buttery flavor that is delicious with vegetables and white sauce.

| 1 | **medium spaghetti squash** |

Vegetable mixture:

1	**tablespoon olive oil**
1	**onion, chopped**
3	**cups sliced mushrooms (about 1/2 pound)**
2	**garlic cloves, minced**
1	**teaspoon basil**
1/2	**teaspoon oregano**
1/2	**teaspoon thyme**
4	**large tomatoes, finely chopped**
1/4	**cup chopped parsley**
1/2	**teaspoon salt**

White sauce:

5	**tablespoons flour**
1 1/2	**cups soy milk or rice milk**
3	**tablespoons nutritional yeast**
1/2	**teaspoon salt**

Cut the squash in half lengthwise, and scoop out the seeds. Place it on a vegetable steamer in a large pot. Cover and steam until tender when pierced with a fork, about 40 minutes.

While the squash cooks, heat the oil in a large skillet and add the onion, mushrooms, garlic, basil, oregano, and thyme. Cook over high heat until the mushrooms are browned, about 7 minutes. Add the tomatoes and chopped parsley and simmer about 10 minutes, until most of the liquid has evaporated. Add salt to taste.

In a separate pan, blend the flour, soy milk, nutritional yeast, and salt. Cook over medium heat, stirring constantly, until thickened.

When the squash is tender and cool enough to handle, use a fork to gently loosen the insides from the shell (leave it in the shell). Place both halves in a baking dish and sprinkle with salt and pepper. Divide the white sauce between the two halves and spread it evenly over the top, then do the same with the vegetable mixture.

Bake at 350°F for 20 minutes. To serve, place on a platter and garnish with parsley.

Per serving: 132 calories; 2 g protein; 20 g carbohydrate; 4 g fat; 186 mg sodium; 0 mg cholesterol

Stuffed Eggplant

Serves 6

One of my students was brave (or foolish) enough to try this recipe on her husband, a confirmed meat-eater and eggplant-hater. He declared it "the best meat I ever ate!"

1	**large eggplant or 3 small eggplants**
1	**tablespoon olive oil**
2	**onions, chopped**
2	**garlic cloves, minced**
2	**bell peppers, diced**
1 1/2	**cups chopped tomatoes**
3	**tablespoons chopped parsley**
1/4	**teaspoon basil**
1/2	**teaspoon salt**
2	**tablespoons Spectrum Naturals Spread or melted margarine**
1/2	**cup walnuts, chopped**
1/2	**cup wheat germ**

Preheat the oven to 350°F. Slice the eggplant(s) in half lengthwise and scoop out the insides, leaving a 1/4-inch thick shell. Place the shells, cut sides down, in an oil-sprayed baking dish and bake until they just begin to soften, about 20 minutes.

Coarsely chop the eggplant flesh. Heat the oil in a large non-stick skillet and add the chopped eggplant, onions, garlic, and bell peppers. Cook over medium heat, stirring often, until the eggplant begins to soften, about 10 minutes (add a small amount of water if necessary to prevent sticking).

Add the tomatoes, parsley, basil, and salt. Cook over medium heat until the eggplant is tender when pierced with a fork, about 10 minutes. Divide the mixture among the eggplant shells.

Mix the Spectrum Spread or melted margarine with the walnuts and wheat germ. Spread evenly over the eggplant shells.

Arrange the shells in one or two baking dishes. Bake until the shells are tender when pierced with a fork, about 45 minutes. Serve with brown rice or Basmati and Wild Rice Pilaf (page 98).

Per serving: 253 calories; 7 g protein; 32 g carbohydrate; 10 g fat; 198 mg sodium; 0 mg cholesterol

Lasagne

Serves 10 to 12

I was never satisfied with vegan lasagne (even my own!) until I added "Vegan Rella", a completely dairy-free cheese sold in natural food stores. It added the richness and body I'd been missing. If you can't locate Vegan Rella, you can substitute another non-dairy cheese, though most other brands contain casein, a dairy derivative.

1/2	cup water
1	tablespoon soy sauce
1	onion, chopped
4	garlic cloves, pressed or minced
2	cups sliced mushrooms (optional)
1	28-ounce can crushed or ground tomatoes
1	6-ounce can tomato paste
3	tablespoons apple juice concentrate
2	teaspoons basil
1	teaspoon oregano
1/2	teaspoon thyme
1/2	teaspoon fennel seeds (optional)
1/4	teaspoon black pepper
1	pound firm tofu, mashed
1/2	teaspoon salt
1/2	teaspoon nutmeg
1/4	teaspoon black pepper
1	10-ounce package frozen chopped spinach, thawed
1	8-ounce package Italian-style Vegan Rella, grated
10-12	lasagne noodles, uncooked

Heat the water and soy sauce in a large skillet and add the onion and garlic. Cook over high heat, stirring frequently, until the onion is soft, about 5 minutes. If you are using the mushrooms, add them and cook another 5 minutes. Add the tomatoes, tomato paste, apple juice concentrate, basil, oregano, thyme, fennel seeds, and 1/4 teaspoon of black pepper. Simmer 15 minutes.

Preheat the oven to 350°F. Combine the mashed tofu, salt, nutmeg, and 1/4 teaspoon of black pepper.

To assemble the lasagne, spread 1 cup of sauce in a 9 x 13-inch (or larger) baking dish. Cover with a layer of uncooked noodles, then with half of the tofu mixture, half the spinach, half the grated Vegan Rella, and half the sauce. Repeat the layers, ending with the sauce. Cover tightly with foil, and bake until the noodles are tender, about 40 minutes. Let stand 10 minutes before serving.

Note: The lasagne can be assembled up to a day in advance, and baked just before serving. The noodles soften while it stands, so the baking time can be reduced to 30 minutes.

Per serving: 189 calories; 10 g protein; 28 g carbohydrate; 4 g fat; 373 mg sodium; 0 mg cholesterol

Manicotti

Serves 8

Tofu makes a delicious creamy filling for manicotti. For the best texture and flavor, be sure to use firm tofu that is very fresh.

1/2	**cup red wine**
1	**onion, chopped**
4	**garlic cloves, pressed or minced**
3	**cups sliced mushrooms (about 1/2 pound)**
1/2	**cup chopped parsley**
1	**28-ounce can crushed or ground tomatoes**
3	**tablespoons apple juice concentrate or 2 teaspoons sugar**
1	**cup water**
1	**teaspoon basil**
1	**teaspoon oregano**
1/2	**teaspoon fennel seeds (optional)**
1/4	**teaspoon black pepper**

1/2	**cup chopped parsley**
1	**garlic clove**
1	**pound firm tofu**
1	**teaspoon basil**
1/2	**teaspoon oregano**
1/2	**teaspoon thyme**
1/2	**teaspoon nutmeg**
1/2	**teaspoon salt**
1/4	**teaspoon black pepper**

8-10   uncooked manicotti shells

Heat the wine in a large pot and add the onion and garlic. Cook until the onion is soft, about five minutes. Add the mushrooms and parsley, then lower the heat slightly, cover and cook until the mushrooms are browned, about 5 minutes. Stir in the tomatoes, apple juice concentrate, water, basil, oregano, fennel seeds, and black pepper. Cover and simmer 15 minutes.

To prepare the filling, finely chop the parsley and garlic in a food processor, then add the tofu, basil, oregano, thyme, nutmeg, salt, and black pepper. Process until very smooth.

Preheat the oven to 350°F. Spread 1 cup of tomato sauce in a 9 x 13-inch (or larger) baking dish. Stuff the uncooked manicotti shells with the tofu mixture and arrange them in the dish. Spread them with the remaining tomato sauce and cover the pan tightly with foil. Bake in the preheated oven until the shells are soft, about 1 hour.

Per manicotti: 164 calories; 9 g protein; 27 g carbohydrate; 2 g fat; 99 mg sodium; 0 mg cholesterol

Refried Beans

Serves 8

These beans are flavorful and satisfying without actually being fried. Serve them with rice and salad, or as a filling for burritos.

11/2	**cups dry pinto beans**
2	**garlic cloves, minced**
11/2	**teaspoons cumin**
1/4	**teaspoon cayenne**
1	**tablespoon olive oil or 1/2 cup water**
1	**onion, chopped**
2	**garlic cloves, minced or crushed**
1	**15-ounce can chopped or crushed tomatoes**
1	**4-ounce can diced chilies**
1/2-1	**teaspoon salt**

Pick through the beans to remove any debris, then rinse and soak in about 6 cups of water for 6 to 8 hours. Discard the soaking water, rinse the beans and place them in a large pot with 4 cups of fresh water, 2 cloves of minced garlic, the cumin and cayenne. Simmer until tender, about 1 hour.

Heat the oil or water in a large skillet and cook the onion and remaining 2 garlic cloves until the onion is soft, about 5 minutes. Stir in the tomatoes and diced chilies. Cook, uncovered, over medium heat for 10 minutes.

Begin adding the cooked beans, along with their liquid, a cup at a time, mashing them as you add them. When all the beans have been added, stir to mix, then cook over low heat, stirring frequently, until thickened. Add salt to taste.

Per serving (with oil): 152 calories; 7 g protein; 27 g carbohydrate; 1.5 g fat; 289 mg sodium; 0 mg cholesterol

Per serving (without oil): 142 calories; 7 g protein; 27 g carbohydrate; 0 g fat; 289 mg sodium; 0 mg cholesterol

Black Bean Chili

Serves 8

Black Bean Chili is great with brown rice or cornbread and a green salad. It also makes a delicious filling for burritos.

2	cups dry black beans
4	cups water
1	large onion, chopped
1	green bell pepper, diced
2	garlic cloves, minced
1	tablespoon cumin seeds
1	tablespoon oregano
1	tablespoon chili powder
1	teaspoon paprika
1	15-ounce can chopped or crushed tomatoes
1	cup chopped cilantro (optional)
1/2-1	teaspoon salt
4	green onions, chopped (including tops)

Rinse the beans and soak them in about 6 cups of water for 6 to 8 hours or overnight.

Pour off the soaking water, then rinse and drain the beans. Place them in a large pot with 4 cups of fresh water, the onion, bell pepper, and garlic.

In a small skillet, toast the cumin seeds, oregano, chili powder, and paprika, stirring constantly, until they just begin to smoke. Be careful not to inhale the fumes, which can be irritating.

Add the toasted spices to the beans and bring to a simmer. Cover and cook until the beans are tender, about 1 1/2 hours. Stir occasionally and add extra water if needed.

When the beans are tender, add the tomatoes and chopped cilantro. Simmer at least 30 minutes (longer cooking enhances the flavor). Add salt to taste. Garnish with chopped green onions.

Per serving: 163 calories; 9 g protein; 30 g carbohydrate; 0 g fat; 140 mg sodium; 0 mg cholesterol

Chili Beans

Serves 6

These chili beans are delicious with cornbread, warm tortillas, or brown rice. A crisp green salad rounds out the meal beautifully. If you have leftover beans, use them to make the Corn Pone on the next page.

1 1/2	**cups dry pinto beans**
4	**cups water**
3	**large garlic cloves, minced**
1/2	**teaspoon ground cumin**
1	**onion chopped**
1	**green bell pepper, diced**
1	**15-ounce can tomato sauce**
1	**cup corn, fresh or frozen**
2	**teaspoons chili powder**
1/8	**teaspoon cayenne (more for spicier beans)**
1/2	**teaspoon salt**

Sort through the beans to remove any debris, then rinse and soak for 6 to 8 hours in about 6 cups of cold water. Discard the soaking water and rinse the beans. Place them in a pot with 4 cups of fresh water, the garlic and cumin. Simmer until tender, about 1 hour.

Heat 1/2 cup of water in a large skillet and cook the onion and bell pepper until the onion is soft, about 5 minutes. Add to the cooked beans, along with the tomato sauce, corn, chili powder, and cayenne. Simmer at least 30 minutes. Add salt to taste.

Crockpot method: Place the soaked beans in a crockpot with the garlic, cumin and 3 cups of boiling water. Set the crockpot on high and cook until the beans are tender, about 3 hours. Add the onion, bell pepper, tomato sauce, corn, chili powder, and cayenne. Continue cooking on high for at least 1 hour. Add salt to taste.

Per serving: 210 calories; 10 g protein; 41 g carbohydrate; 0 g fat; 218 mg sodium; 0 mg cholesterol

Corn Pone

Serves 10

Are you wondering what to do with leftover chili beans? Give Corn Pone a try!   Spicy beans topped with a golden cornbread crust make a truly marvelous meal.

6	**cups chili beans with their juice**
2	**cups soy milk or rice milk**
2	**tablespoons vinegar**
2	**cups corn meal**
2	**teaspoons baking soda**
1/2	**teaspoon salt**
2	**tablespoons oil**

Heat the chili beans on the stovetop or in a microwave until steamy and hot, then spread them evenly in a 9 x 13-inch baking dish.

Preheat the oven to 400°F. Combine the soy milk or rice milk with the vinegar.

Mix the cornmeal, baking soda, and salt in a large bowl, then add the oil and milk-vinegar mixture. Stir to dissolve any lumps then pour over the hot beans. Bake until the cornbread is set and golden brown, about 30 minutes.

Per serving: 268 calories; 9 g protein; 49 g carbohydrate; 3.5 g fat; 410 mg sodium; 0 mg cholesterol

Pueblo Pie

Serves 10

Pueblo Pie is a bit like a Mexican lasagne, with layers of tortillas, garbanzo cheeze, chili beans, corn, and a spicy tomato sauce. Serve it with a green salad for a very satisfying meal.

1/2	cup water
1	large onion, chopped
1	tablespoon minced garlic (about 4 large cloves)
1	28-ounce can crushed tomatoes
4	teaspoons chili powder
2	teaspoons cumin
2/3	cup textured vegetable protein (TVP)
2/3	cup water
1	15-ounce can garbanzo beans, drained
1/2	cup roasted red pepper (about 2 peppers)
3	tablespoons tahini
3	tablespoons lemon juice
12	corn tortillas, torn in half
2	15-ounce cans vegetarian chili beans
1	cup chopped green onions
1-2	cups corn, fresh or frozen

Heat 1/2 cup of water in a large pot or skillet and cook the onion and garlic until soft, about 5 minutes. Add the tomatoes, chili powder, cumin, textured vegetable protein, and 2/3 cup of water. Simmer over medium heat 5 minutes.

Process the garbanzo beans, roasted peppers, tahini, and lemon juice in a food processor or blender until very smooth.

Preheat the oven to 350°F.

Spread about 1/2 cup of the tomato sauce in the bottom of a 9 x 13-inch (or larger) baking dish. Cover with a layer of tortillas, then spread with a third of the garbanzo bean mixture, using your fingers to hold the tortillas in place. Sprinkle with a third of the chili beans, green onions, and corn. Spread about 1 cup of tomato sauce over the top. Repeat the layers twice, ending with the tomato sauce. Make sure all the tortillas are covered. Bake for 20 minutes.

Per serving: 282 calories; 13 g protein; 47 g carbohydrate; 4 g fat; 347 mg sodium; 0 mg cholesterol

Broccoli Burritos

Makes 6 burritos

This is absolutely the most delicious way I know of eating broccoli: rolled in a flour tortilla with a tangy garbanzo spread. Look for roasted red peppers in jars in your supermarket. Tahini (sesame butter) is sold in natural food stores, ethnic markets, and many supermarkets.

2-3	**stalks of broccoli (about 2 cups chopped)**
1	**15-ounce can garbanzo beans**
1/2	**cup roasted red peppers**
2	**tablespoons tahini**
3	**tablespoons lemon juice**
6	**flour tortillas**
6	**tablespoons salsa (or more to taste)**

Cut or break the broccoli into florets. Peel the stalks and cut them into 1/2-inch thick rounds. Steam over boiling water until just barely tender, about 5 minutes.

Drain the garbanzo beans and place them in a food processor with the peppers, tahini, and lemon juice. Process until completely smooth.

Spread about 1/4 cup of the garbanzo mixture on a tortilla and place it in a large heated skillet. Heat it until the tortilla is warm and soft, about 2 minutes. Arrange a line of cooked broccoli down the center of the tortilla, then sprinkle with salsa. Fold the bottom of the tortilla toward the center, then starting on one side, roll the tortilla around the filling. Repeat with remaining tortillas.

Per burrito: 244 calories; 9 g protein; 39 g carbohydrate; 5 g fat; 130 mg sodium; 0 mg cholesterol

Truly Terrific Tacos

Makes 10 to 12 tacos

People often ask if I missed meat when I became a vegetarian. My answer is an emphatic "Definitely not!" But I did miss tacos . . . until I discovered textured vegetable protein, a soyfood that makes one of the tastiest tacos around. Look for textured vegetable protein (or TVP) in natural food stores and some supermarkets.

1	cup water
1	small onion, chopped
2	garlic cloves, minced or crushed
1/2	small bell pepper, finely diced
3/4	cup textured vegetable protein
1	cup tomato sauce
2	teaspoons chili powder
1/2	teaspoon cumin
1/4	teaspoon oregano
1	tablespoon nutritional yeast (optional)
1	tablespoon soy sauce
12	corn tortillas
1	cup shredded romaine lettuce
4	green onions, sliced
1	medium tomato, diced
1	avocado, cut into strips (optional)
1/2	cup salsa or taco sauce

Heat the water in a large pan and cook the onion, garlic, and bell pepper until the onion is soft, about 5 minutes.

Add the textured vegetable protein, tomato sauce, chili powder, cumin, oregano, nutritional yeast if you are using it, and soy sauce. Cook over low heat until the mixture is fairly dry, about 8 minutes.

Heat a tortilla in a heavy skillet, flipping it from side to side until it is soft and pliable. Place a small amount of the filling along the center and fold the tortilla over it. Cook about 1 minute on each side. Garnish with lettuce, onions, tomato, avocado, and salsa.

Per taco: 105 calories; 6 g protein; 18 g carbohydrate; 1 g fat; 63 mg sodium; 0 mg cholesterol

Baked Beans

Serves 8

These beans may be "baked," on the stovetop, in the oven, or in a crockpot. The longer they cook, the more delicious they become.

21/2	**cups dried navy beans (or other small white beans)**
1	**onion, chopped**
1	**15-ounce can tomato sauce**
1/2	**cup molasses**
2	**teaspoons stone ground or Dijon mustard**
2	**tablespoons vinegar**
1/2	**teaspoon garlic powder or granules**
1-2	**teaspoons salt**

Rinse the beans thoroughly and soak in 6 cups of water for 6 to 8 hours. Discard the soaking water and place the beans and chopped onion in a pot with enough water to cover the beans with 1 inch of water. Bring to a simmer, then cover and cook until the beans are tender, 2 to 3 hours.

Add the tomato sauce, molasses, mustard, vinegar, and garlic powder or granules. Cook, loosely covered, over very low heat for 1 to 2 hours. Or, transfer to an ovenproof dish and bake at 350°F for 2 to 3 hours. Add salt to taste.

Crockpot variation: Place the cooked beans into a crockpot with all the remaining ingredients. Cover and cook on high for 2 to 3 hours.

Per serving: 258 calories; 10 g protein; 52 g carbohydrate; 0 g fat; 327 mg sodium; 0 mg cholesterol

Cabbage Rolls

Serves 8 to 10

Although this recipe has several ingredients and steps, it really isn't difficult to prepare, and everything comes together so deliciously in the end that it's well worth the effort. You could save some time by using a commercially prepared marinara sauce.

1	head green cabbage

Filling:

1/2	cup water or vegetable stock
1	onion, chopped
1	garlic clove, crushed
2 1/2	cups sliced mushrooms (about 1/2 pound)
1/2	teaspoon paprika
1/8	teaspoon black pepper
1/8	teaspoon cayenne
3	cups cooked brown rice (see page 96)
1/4	cup raisins
1/4	cup pine nuts

Sauce:

1/2	cup water or vegetable stock
1	small onion, chopped
1	garlic clove, crushed
1	15-ounce can crushed or ground tomatoes
1/4	teaspoon each: basil, oregano, fennel seeds
1/8	teaspoon each: thyme, marjoram, black pepper

Wash the cabbage and remove the core. Steam the cabbage in a covered pot until it is quite soft, about 20 minutes. Remove it from the pot. When it is cool enough to handle, carefully peel off 12 large leaves and set aside. Chop enough of the remaining cabbage to make 1 cup.

To prepare the filling, heat 1/2 cup of water and cook the onion until it is soft, about 5 minutes. Add the garlic and mushrooms. Cook for 5 minutes, stirring occasionally. Stir in paprika, black pepper, and cayenne. Remove from the heat and stir in the cooked rice, raisins, pine nuts, and chopped cabbage. Set aside.

To prepare the sauce, heat 1/2 cup of water or stock, then add the onion and garlic. Cook until the onion is soft, about 5 minutes. Add the tomatoes, basil, oregano, fennel seeds, thyme, marjoram, and black pepper. Simmer over medium heat until the flavors are blended, about 25 minutes.

Preheat the oven to 350°F. To assemble, divide the filling among the 12 cabbage leaves. Roll up each leaf, starting at the core end and tucking in the edges. Arrange in a 9 x 13-inch (or larger) baking dish, then pour the sauce evenly over the top. Bake for 25 minutes.

Per serving: 112 calories; 3 g protein; 24 g carbohydrate; 0 g fat; 130 mg sodium; 0 mg cholesterol

Mjeddrah (Middle Eastern Lentils and Rice)

Serves 8

You should try this recipe even if you can't pronounce it! Mjeddrah (pronounced "mu-jed-rah") is a traditional Middle Eastern dish consisting of lentils and rice topped with a green salad and lemon vinaigrette. The combination of the peppery lentils with the cool salad and tart vinaigrette is delightful.

1	tablespoon olive oil
2	large onions, coarsely chopped
3/4	cup brown rice
1 1/2	teaspoons salt
1 1/2	cups lentils, rinsed
4	cups boiling water
4-6	cups leaf lettuce or salad mix
1-2	tomatoes, cut into wedges
2-3	green onions, chopped
1	cucumber, thinly sliced
1	avocado, sliced
2	tablespoons olive oil
2	tablespoons lemon juice
1	teaspoon sugar or other sweetener
1/2	teaspoon paprika
1/4	teaspoon dry mustard
1	garlic clove, pressed
1/4	teaspoon salt

Heat 1 tablespoon of olive oil in a large pot and sauté the onions until soft, about 5 minutes. Add the rice and 1 1/2 teaspoons of salt. Cook for 3 minutes. Stir in the lentils and boiling water. Bring to a simmer, then cover and cook until the rice and lentils are tender, about 50 minutes.

While the lentil mixture is cooking, prepare a generous green salad using leaf lettuce or salad mix, tomatoes, green onions, cucumber, and avocado. Feel free to add any other ingredients you'd enjoy in the salad.

Combine 2 tablespoons olive oil with the lemon juice, sugar, paprika, dry mustard, garlic, and salt. Mix well then pour over the salad. Toss to mix.

To serve, place some of the lentil mixture on each plate and top with a generous serving of salad.

Per serving: 214 calories; 8 g protein; 32 g carbohydrate; 5 g fat; 470 mg sodium; 0 mg cholesterol

Tofu Burgers

Makes 8 burgers

These burgers are quick and easy to make. The ingredients can be mixed in advance and stored in the refrigerator for up to a week. Form and cook the patties as needed. Or you can cook all the patties at one time, then store them in the refrigerator and reheat them in a toaster oven or microwave. If you want to grill the burgers, precook the patties before putting them on the grill.

1	**pound firm tofu, mashed**
1/2	**cup quick-cooking rolled oats**
1	**slice whole wheat bread, finely crumbled**
1	**small onion, finely chopped or 2 tablespoons onion powder**
1 1/2	**tablespoons finely chopped parsley**
3	**tablespoons soy sauce**
1	**teaspoon garlic powder or granules**
1/2	**teaspoon each: basil, oregano, cumin**
8	**whole wheat burger buns**
8	**lettuce leaves**
8	**tomato slices**
8	**red onion slices**

Nayonaise, mustard, ketchup, barbecue sauce, etc.

Mix the tofu with the rolled oats, bread crumbs, chopped onion, parsley, soy sauce, and seasonings. Knead for a minute or so, until the mixture holds together. Shape into 8 patties. Lightly spray a large skillet (preferably nonstick) with oil, then add the patties and brown on both sides.

Toast the buns, garnish them with all your favorite trimmings, then top it off with a tofu patty.

Baked version: Place the tofu patties on an oil-sprayed baking sheet. Bake at 350°F until lightly browned, about 25 minutes.

Per serving: 180 calories; 9 g protein; 30 g carbohydrate; 2.5 g fat; 483 mg sodium; 0 mg cholesterol

Sloppy Joes

Serves 4

These Sloppy Joes are made with textured vegetable protein (TVP) a "meaty" soyfood available in natural food stores.

11/2	cups water
1	large onion, finely chopped
1	bell pepper, finely diced
1	cup textured vegetable protein
1	15-ounce can tomato sauce
1	tablespoon sugar or other sweetener
1	teaspoon chili powder
1	teaspoon garlic powder or granules
2	tablespoons cider vinegar
1	tablespoon soy sauce
1	teaspoon stone ground or Dijon mustard
4	whole wheat burger buns

Heat 1/2 cup of the water in a large pot, then add the chopped onion and bell pepper. Cook until the onion is soft, about 5 minutes. Add the remaining 1 cup of water, the textured vegetable protein, tomato sauce, sugar, chili powder, garlic powder, cider vinegar, soy sauce, and mustard. Cook over medium heat, stirring frequently, for 10 minutes.

Split the buns and warm them in a toaster oven. Top with a serving of sauce.

Per serving: 158 calories; 14 g protein; 24 g carbohydrate; 1 g fat; 230 mg sodium; 0 mg cholesterol

Tofu Croquettes

Makes about 25 croquettes

Serve these croquettes with barbecue sauce or sweet and sour sauce. The leftovers make wonderful snacks and are perfect for brown bag lunches.

3	cups cooked brown rice (see page 96)
10	ounces firm tofu, mashed
1	small onion, finely chopped
1/2	cup finely chopped parsley
1/2	cup tahini
2	tablespoons soy sauce

Combine the cooked rice, tofu, onion, parsley, tahini, and soy sauce. Mix well. Form into walnut-sized balls and place on a greased baking sheet. Bake at 350°F until browned, about 25 minutes.

Tofu Pot Pie

Serves 8

This hearty pot pie takes a bit of time to prepare, but it's well worth the effort. For a lower-fat, less time-consuming version, you can eliminate the crust and serve the filling as a stew over cooked brown rice.

1	tablespoon olive oil
1	large onion, chopped
2	carrots, diced
3	stalks celery, thinly sliced
4	cups sliced mushrooms
1	pound very firm tofu, cut into 1/4-inch cubes
1/4	cup unbleached flour
2	cups water
1	teaspoon salt
1	teaspoon garlic powder or granules
1	teaspoon sage
1/2	teaspoon thyme
1/2	teaspoon paprika
1/4	teaspoon black pepper
1	cup peas, fresh or frozen
1	10-inch pie crust (recipe on page 148)

Heat the oil in a large nonstick skillet and cook the onion until soft, about 5 minutes. Add the carrots, celery, and mushrooms. Lower the heat slightly, then cover and cook until the mushrooms are browned and the carrots tender, stirring occasionally, about 7 minutes. Remove the vegetables from the skillet and set them aside.

Add the tofu cubes to the skillet and cook, turning gently with a spatula, until golden brown, about 3 minutes.

Combine the flour, water, salt, garlic powder, sage, thyme, paprika, and black pepper in a small bowl. Stir to mix. Add to the tofu, stirring gently over medium heat until thickened to the consistency of gravy. Remove from the heat and stir in the onion mixture and peas.

Preheat the oven to 400°F. Spread the tofu-vegetable mixture in a 10-inch unbaked pie crust. Cover with the top crust, pinching the edges of the top and bottom crusts together. Cut slits in the top to allow steam to escape. Bake in the preheated oven for 20 minutes, then reduce the heat to 350°F. Bake 20 to 30 minutes longer, until the crust is nicely browned.

Per serving: 260 calories; 12 g protein; 32 g carbohydrate; 8 g fat; 410 mg sodium; 0 mg cholesterol

Neat Loaf

Serves 8 to 10

For a truly traditional meal, try serving Neat Loaf with Mashed Potatoes and Gravy (page 91), and Green Beans with Toasted Almonds (page 88). If you have any leftover, try slicing it for delicious Neat Loaf sandwiches. In order for the mixture to hold together, the vegetables should be chopped as finely as possible. This is easily accomplished with a food processor.

2	cups cooked brown rice (see page 96)
1	cup walnuts, finely chopped
1	cup chopped mushrooms
1	onion, finely chopped
1/2	medium bell pepper, finely chopped
2	medium carrots, shredded or finely chopped
1	cup wheat germ
1	cup quick-cooking rolled oats
1/2	teaspoon each: thyme, marjoram, sage
2	tablespoons soy sauce
2	tablespoons stone ground or Dijon mustard

barbecue sauce or ketchup

Preheat the oven to 350°F. Combine all the ingredients except the barbecue sauce or ketchup. Mix for 2 minutes with a large spoon. This will help bind it together. Pat into an oil-sprayed 5 x 9-inch loaf pan and top with barbecue sauce or ketchup. Bake for 60 minutes. Let stand for 10 minutes before serving.

Per serving: 204 calories; 9 g protein; 19 g carbohydrate; 9 g fat; 248 mg sodium; 0 mg cholesterol

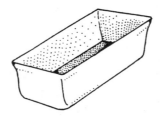

Foods from India

India is well known for its long history of vegetarianism among many of the country's inhabitants. Even among non-vegetarians, meat (and especially red meat) plays a far less prominent role than in the United States and other western cultures. A typical Indian meal provides a tantalizing array of flavors and textures, usually including dal (a bean dish), rice, and an assortment of vegetables. For example, try the Masoor Dal on this page with Pilau (page 97), Quick Confetti Rice (page 96), or Couscous (page 102). Add the Curried Mushrooms with Chickpeas (page 132) and Apple Chutney (page 68) for a real Indian feast!

Masoor Dal (Red Lentil Curry)

Serves 4 to 6

"Dal" is the Indian term for legumes—beans , lentils, and peas—and refers to any dish which consists primarily of legumes. Masoor dal is a small, bright orange lentil available in natural food stores and ethnic markets. If you can't locate masoor dal, yellow split peas may be substituted. This dish is extremely easy to make, and cooks quickly. The consistency can range from that of a thick pea soup to refried beans, depending on your preference. Simply increase the cooking time for a thicker dal.

1	**cup masoor dal**
3	**cups water**
1/2	**teaspoon salt**
1	**tablespoon oil**
1	**teaspoon mustard seeds**
1/4	**teaspoon turmeric**
1/4	**teaspoon cumin**
1/4	**teaspoon coriander**
1/4	**teaspoon ginger**
1/8	**teaspoon cayenne**

Sort through the masoor dal and pick out any debris, then rinse it and put it in a pot. Add the water and salt and bring to a simmer. Cook until completely tender, 15 to 20 minutes (45 minutes for yellow split peas).

In a large skillet, heat the oil and add the mustard seeds, turmeric, cumin, coriander, ginger, and cayenne. Cook over medium heat until the mustard seeds begin to pop (be careful not to inhale the fumes, as these can be irritating).

Remove the skillet from the heat and slowly add the cooked dal. Be careful, it may splatter. Return the skillet to the heat and simmer gently, stirring occasionally until the dal is thickened.

Per serving: 116 calories; 6 g protein; 18 g carbohydrate; 2 g fat; 179 mg sodium; 0 mg cholesterol

Lentil Dal

Serves 8

Common lentils, found in any grocery store, make a delicious, spicy dal. Serve with basmati rice, couscous, or chapatis.

1	**tablespoon oil**
2	**large onions, chopped**
4	**garlic cloves, crushed or minced**
2	**teaspoons cumin seeds**
2	**teaspoons coriander**
1	**teaspoon turmeric**
1/2	**teaspoon cayenne**
2	**cups lentils, rinsed**
51/2	**cups boiling water**
1	**teaspoon salt**

Heat the oil in a pot, then add the onions and garlic. Cook until soft, about 5 minutes.

Add the cumin seeds, coriander, turmeric, and cayenne. Cook another minute (be careful not to inhale the fumes).

Add the lentils and boiling water. Cover and simmer until the lentils are tender, about 1 hour. Stir occasionally while cooking. If the mixture becomes too thick, add a bit more water. Add salt to taste.

Per serving: 173 calories;10 g protein; 28 g carbohydrate; 2 g fat; 270 mg sodium; 0 mg cholesterol

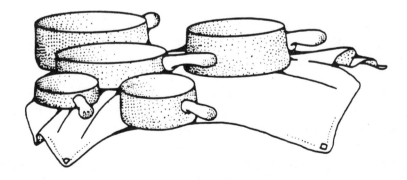

Yellow Split Pea Dal

Serves 6 to 8

1 1/2	cups yellow split peas
1	teaspoon salt
4	cups water
1	tablespoon oil
1	teaspoon cumin seeds
1	teaspoon turmeric
1/2	teaspoon mustard seeds
1/4	teaspoon cinnamon
1/4	teaspoon ginger
1/4	teaspoon coriander
1/4	teaspoon cayenne

Rinse the peas and put them in a pot with the salt and water. Cover and simmer until tender, about 1 hour.

Heat the oil in a large skillet and add the spices to it. Cook for a few minutes, stirring constantly, then remove the pan from the heat.

Pour in the cooked peas (be careful, they may splatter). Return the pan to the heat and simmer, stirring often, until the dal is fairly thick.

Per serving: 124 calories; 7 g protein; 20 g carbohydrate; 2 g fat; 268 mg sodium; 0 mg cholesterol

Curried Mushrooms and Chickpeas

Serves 8

The original version of this recipe was given to me by my dear friend Inder Singh. It called for 1 to 2 teaspoons of cayenne and was fiery indeed! I have reduced the amount of cayenne (much to Inder's dismay) to 1/2 teaspoon. If the dish is still too hot for your taste, decrease the cayenne to 1/4 teaspoon. If, like Inder, you find this recipe too mild, add more cayenne. Serve with dal and pilau or couscous.

1	**tablespoon oil or 1/2 cup water**
2	**large onions, chopped**
1 1/2	**pounds mushrooms, sliced**
1 1/2	**tablespoons whole cumin seeds**
1	**28-ounce can crushed or ground tomatoes**
1	**15-ounce can garbanzo beans, drained**
1	**teaspoon turmeric**
1	**teaspoon coriander**
1/2	**teaspoon cayenne**
1/2	**teaspoon ginger**
1/2	**teaspoon salt**

Heat the oil or water in a large pot, then add the onions and cook over high heat until soft, about 5 minutes. Add the mushrooms and cumin seeds and continue cooking until the mushrooms are browned, about 5 minutes.

Add the tomatoes, garbanzo beans, turmeric, coriander, cayenne, and ginger. Cook 30 minutes or longer, until the mushrooms are tender and the flavors are well blended. Add salt to taste.

Per serving (with oil): 127 calories; 5 g protein; 20 g carbohydrate; 2 g fat; 150 mg sodium;
                         0 mg cholesterol

Per serving (without oil): 112 calories; 5 g protein; 20 g carbohydrate; 1 g fat; 150 mg sodium;
                         0 mg cholesterol

DESSERTS
&
BEVERAGES

Until he extends the circle of his compassion to all living things,
man will not himself find peace.
Albert Schweitzer

Berry Cobbler

Serves 9

The "birth" of this recipe marked the end of my berry pie-making days. It is so much easier to make, much lower in fat, and tastes absolutely wonderful. For a real treat, top the hot cobbler with a spoonful of non-dairy frozen dessert.

5-6	cups fresh or frozen berries (boysenberries, blackberries, raspberries, or a mixture of these)
3	tablespoons whole wheat pastry flour
1/2	cup sugar or other sweetener
1	cup whole wheat pastry flour
2	tablespoons sugar or other sweetener
11/2	teaspoons baking powder
1/4	teaspoon salt
2	tablespoons vegetable oil
1/2	cup soy milk or rice milk

Preheat the oven to 400°F. Spread the berries in a 9 x 9-inch baking dish and mix them with 3 tablespoons of flour and 1/2 cup of sugar.

In a separate bowl, mix 1 cup of flour and 2 tablespoons of sugar with the baking powder and salt. Add the oil and mix it with a fork or your fingers until the mixture resembles coarse corn meal. Add the soy milk or rice milk and stir to mix. Spread over the berries (don't worry if they're not completely covered), then bake until golden brown, about 25 minutes.

Per serving: 166 calories; 3 g protein; 32 g carbohydrate; 3 g fat; 67 mg sodium; 0 mg cholesterol

Peach Cobbler

Serves 9

Fresh peaches are the essence of summertime, and this is such a delicious way to eat them. If you get a yearning for this cobbler in the middle of winter, use frozen peaches instead.

1/2	**cup sugar or other sweetener**
2	**tablespoons cornstarch or arrowroot powder**
1	**cup water**
5	**cups sliced peaches, fresh or frozen**
1/2	**teaspoon cinnamon**
1 1/4	**cups whole wheat pastry flour**
2	**tablespoons sugar**
1 1/2	**teaspoons baking powder**
1/4	**teaspoon salt**
2	**tablespoons vegetable oil**
1/2	**cup soy milk or rice milk**

Mix the sugar and cornstarch in a saucepan, then stir in the water and peaches. Bring to a boil and cook over medium-high heat, stirring constantly, until the sauce is clear and thick. Pour into a 9 x 9-inch baking dish, and sprinkle with the cinnamon.

Preheat the oven to 400°F. Mix the flour, 2 tablespoons of sugar, baking powder, and salt in a large bowl. Add the oil and work it into the flour with a fork or with your fingers until it resembles coarse cornmeal. Stir in the soy milk or rice milk, then drop by spoonfuls onto the hot peach mixture. Bake until golden brown, about 25 minutes.

Per serving: 196 calories; 3 g protein; 38 g carbohydrate; 3 g fat; 73 mg sodium; 0 mg cholesterol

Cranberry Apple Crisp

Serves 9

Walnuts and rolled oats make a delicious topping for this colorful crisp.

3	tart green apples, peeled and cored
3	tablespoons lemon juice
1	tablespoon sugar
1	teaspoon cinnamon
1	cup fresh or dried cranberries
1 1/2	cups quick-cooking rolled oats
3/4	cup walnuts, finely chopped
1/3	cup maple syrup
1	teaspoon vanilla
1/4	teaspoon salt

Slice the apples thinly and spread them in a 9 x 9-inch baking dish. Sprinkle with lemon juice, sugar, cinnamon, and the cranberries.

Preheat the oven to 350°F. Combine the rolled oats, walnuts, maple syrup, vanilla, and salt in a bowl. Stir to mix, then spread evenly over the apples. Bake until the apples are tender when pierced with a knife, about 35 minutes. Let stand 5 to 10 minutes before serving.

Per serving: 187 calories; 4 g protein; 28 g carbohydrate; 6 g fat; 62 mg sodium; 0 mg cholesterol

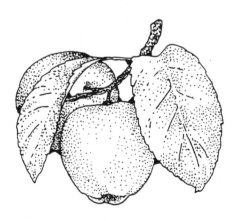

Poached Pears

Serves 4

Poached pears are attractive, delicious, and deceptively easy to prepare. For a real treat, serve them with a non-dairy frozen dessert like Tofutti or Rice Dream.

2	**large ripe pears**
1/2	**cup apple juice concentrate**
1/2	**cup white wine or water**
1	**bag Celestial Seasonings Harvest Spice tea** **or 1/2 teaspoon cinnamon**
1	**pint Tofutti, Rice Dream or other frozen dessert (optional)**

Peel the pears, cut them in half, and remove the cores. Place the pears in a saucepan. Mix the apple juice concentrate with the wine or water, then pour the mixture over the pears. Add the tea bag or cinnamon. Bring to a simmer and cook until the pears are tender when pierced with a fork, 15 to 20 minutes.

Remove the pears from the pan and place them into serving dishes. Set aside.

Remove the tea bag from the pan and continue to simmer the juice until it is decreased by half, about 5 minutes. Pour it over the pears. Top with a scoop of non-dairy frozen dessert if desired.

Per serving: 135 calories; 1 g protein; 31 g carbohydrate; 0 g fat; 13 mg sodium; 0 mg cholesterol

Baked Apples

Serves 4

Baked apples are simple to prepare and make a delicious dessert.

4	**large, tart apples**
3-5	**pitted dates, chopped**
1	**teaspoon cinnamon**

Preheat the oven to 350°F. Wash the apples and remove the cores to within a quarter-inch of the bottom of each apple. Combine the pitted dates and cinnamon and mix well. Stuff the apples with this mixture, then place them in a baking dish filled with 1/4 inch of hot water. Bake until tender, 40 to 60 minutes. Serve hot or chilled.

Per serving: 124 calories; 0.5 g protein; 29 g carbohydrate; 0 g fat; 0 mg sodium; 0 mg cholesterol

Ginger Pear Custard

Serves 8

These pears are topped with a tasty tofu custard. Be sure to use fresh tofu (check the expiration date on the package).

4	large firm pears, thinly sliced
1/4	cup sugar or other sweetener
2	tablespoons unbleached flour
1	tablespoon lemon juice
1/2	teaspoon cinnamon
1/2	teaspoon ginger
1/4	teaspoon salt
1	pound very fresh firm tofu
1/2	cup maple syrup
1/3	cup frozen orange juice concentrate
2	teaspoons vanilla
2	teaspoons lemon juice
1/2	teaspoon cinnamon
1/2	teaspoon ginger
1/4	teaspoon salt

Preheat the oven to 300°F. Place the sliced pears in a large bowl, then sprinkle with the sugar, flour, lemon juice, cinnamon, ginger, and salt. Toss to mix then spread in a 9-inch square baking dish.

Combine the tofu, maple syrup, orange juice concentrate, vanilla, lemon juice, cinnamon, ginger, and salt in a blender. Blend until completely smooth, using a rubber spatula to scrape down the sides of the blender.

Pour the blended ingredients evenly over the pears and bake for 1 hour. Serve warm or chilled.

Per serving: 178 calories; 6 g protein; 35 g carbohydrate; 1 g fat; 126 mg sodium; 0 mg cholesterol

Oatmeal Cookies

Makes 30 2-inch cookies

This recipe is dedicated with love to my mother who has always had a passion for oatmeal cookies.

1	cup unbleached or whole wheat pastry flour
1/2	teaspoon cinnamon
1/2	teaspoon baking soda
1/2	teaspoon baking powder
1/4	teaspoon salt
1/2	cup sugar or other sweetener
1/3	cup vegetable oil
1/4	cup molasses
1	teaspoon vanilla
1 1/2	cups rolled oats
1/4	cup soy milk or rice milk
1/2	cup raisins
1/2	cup walnuts, chopped (optional)

Preheat the oven to 350°F. Mix the flour, cinnamon, baking soda, baking powder, and salt in a large bowl.

In a separate bowl, mix the sugar, oil, molasses, and vanilla until smooth. Add the flour mixture, along with the rolled oats, soy milk or rice milk, raisins, and walnuts. Mix well.

Drop by rounded tablespoonfuls onto an oil-sprayed cookie sheet, leaving room for the cookies to spread. Bake at 350°F until lightly browned, 12 to 15 minutes. Transfer to a rack to cool, then store in an airtight container.

Per cookie: 89 calories; 1 g protein; 16 g carbohydrate; 2 g fat; 34 mg sodium; 0 mg cholesterol

Ginger Crinkle Cookies

Makes 30 2-inch cookies

This recipe was my very first cooking adventure. It came from a children's magazine and was love at first bite. I have since modified it to make it eggless and dairy-free.

2	**cups unbleached or whole wheat pastry flour**
2	**teaspoons baking powder**
2	**teaspoons ginger**
2	**teaspoons cinnamon**
1/2	**teaspoon salt**
1/2	**cup Spectrum Naturals Spread or margarine**
3/4	**cup sugar or other sweetener**
1/4	**cup molasses**
3	**tablespoons water**

Stir the flour, baking powder, ginger, cinnamon, and salt together in a small bowl. In a large bowl, cream the Spectrum Spread or margarine and sugar, then add the molasses and water. Beat smooth. Add the flour mixture, and mix thoroughly.

Preheat the oven to 350°F. Roll the dough into walnut-sized balls. Place them on an oil-sprayed cookie sheet about 2 inches apart. Bake until golden brown, 8 to 10 minutes. Transfer to a rack to cool. Store in an airtight container.

Per cookie: 71 calories; 1 g protein; 12 g carbohydrate; 2 g fat; 64 mg sodium; 0 mg cholesterol

Pecan Drops

Makes 30 1-inch cookies

These cookies are simply delicious, and easy to make if you use a food processor.

2	**cups pecans**
1	**teaspoon finely grated orange peel**
1	**cup pitted moist dates**
30	**pecan halves**

Preheat the oven to 325°F. Grind the pecans and orange peel in a food processor until the pecans are coarsely chopped. Add the dates and process until everything is uniformly mixed and a ball of dough forms. Roll the dough into walnut-sized balls and place on an ungreased baking sheet; they will not spread, so they can be placed close together. Press a pecan half onto the top of each.

Place the baking sheet in the upper third of the oven to prevent the bottoms from burning. Bake for 12 to 15 minutes, until bottoms are lightly browned.

Per cookie: 73 calories; 1 g protein; 6 g carbohydrate; 5 g fat; 0 mg sodium; 0 mg cholesterol

Pumpkin Spice Cookies

Makes 21 3-inch cookies

These cookies are plump and moist.

2	cups whole wheat pastry flour
1/2	cup sugar or other sweetener
2	teaspoons baking powder
1/2	teaspoon baking soda
1/2	teaspoon salt
1/2	teaspoon cinnamon
1/4	teaspoon nutmeg
1	cup pumpkin
1/2	cup soy milk or rice milk
1/2	cup raisins
1/2	cup chopped pecans or walnuts (optional)

Preheat the oven to 350°F. Mix the flour, sugar, baking powder, baking soda, salt, cinnamon, and nutmeg together in a large bowl. Add the pumpkin, soy milk or rice milk, raisins, and nuts. Mix completely, then drop by tablespoonfuls onto an oil-sprayed baking sheet. Bake 15 minutes, until the bottoms are lightly browned. Carefully remove from the baking sheet with a spatula and place on a rack to cool. Store in an airtight container.

Per cookie (with nuts): 90 calories; 3 g protein; 15 g carbohydrate; 2 g fat; 116 mg sodium; 0 mg cholesterol

Per cookie (without nuts): 68 calories; 2 g protein; 15 g carbohydrate; 0 g fat; 116 mg sodium; 0 mg cholesterol

Sesame Bars

Makes 48 bars

These eggless, dairyless bars are chewy and satisfying, and the sesame seeds and tahini supply calcium. It is important to time the cooking of the barley malt (or corn syrup) carefully; if it boils longer than 2 minutes the bars will be hard like peanut brittle.

11/2	**cups unhulled sesame seeds**
3/4	**cup unsweetened shredded coconut**
1/4	**cup raw wheat germ**
1	**cup barley malt or corn syrup**
1/2	**cup peanut butter**
1/4	**cup tahini (sesame seed butter)**

Preheat the oven to 350°F. Mix the sesame seeds, coconut and wheat germ together in a 9 x 13-inch baking dish. Bake until lightly browned, stirring occasionally. This will take about 10 minutes.

In a large saucepan, bring the barley malt or corn syrup to a boil over high heat. Lower the heat slightly and boil for 2 minutes. Remove from the heat and stir in the peanut butter and tahini. Mix well. Add the toasted ingredients and mix completely.

Spread evenly in an oil-sprayed 9 x 13-inch baking dish, smoothing the top with a rubber spatula. Allow to cool slightly then cut into 36 bars and remove from pan.

Per bar: 93 calories; 2 g protein; 8 g carbohydrate; 6 g fat; 8 mg sodium; 0 mg cholesterol

Gingerbread

Makes one 9 x 9-inch gingerbread

You'll find it hard to believe that this delicious gingerbread contains no added fat. Try serving it with hot applesauce for a real treat.

1/2	**cup raisins**
1/2	**cup chopped pitted dates**
13/4	**cups water**
3/4	**cup sugar or other sweetener**
1/2	**teaspoon salt**
2	**teaspoons cinnamon**
1	**teaspoon ginger**
3/4	**teaspoon nutmeg**
1/4	**teaspoon cloves**
2	**cups whole wheat pastry flour**
1	**teaspoon baking soda**
1	**teaspoon baking powder**

Combine the raisins, dates and water in a saucepan. Add the sugar, salt, cinnamon, ginger, nutmeg, and cloves. Bring to a boil. Boil for 2 minutes, then remove from the heat and cool completely (This is very important!).

Preheat the oven to 350°F. Stir the flour, baking soda and baking powder together in a large bowl. Add the cooled fruit mixture and stir just enough to mix. Spread evenly into a 9 x 9-inch pan which has been misted with a vegetable oil spray. Bake in the preheated oven for 30 minutes, until a toothpick inserted into the center comes out clean.

Per 3-inch piece: 207 calories; 4 g protein; 48 g carbohydrate; 0 g fat; 215 mg sodium;
0 mg cholesterol

Carrot Cake

Serves 12

This delicious carrot cake is made without eggs, and contains half of the oil used in traditional recipes.

2	**cups grated carrots**
1 1/2	**cups raisins**
2	**cups water**
1/2	**cup oil**
1 1/4	**cups maple syrup**
1 1/2	**teaspoons cinnamon**
1 1/2	**teaspoons allspice**
1/2	**teaspoon cloves**
1/2	**teaspoon salt**
3	**cups unbleached or whole wheat pastry flour**
1 1/2	**teaspoons baking soda**
3/4	**cup chopped walnuts**

Combine the grated carrots, raisins, and water in a saucepan over medium heat. Simmer for 10 minutes. Add the oil, maple syrup, cinnamon, allspice, cloves, and salt. Cool completely (this is important).

Preheat the oven to 350°F. Stir the flour, soda and walnuts together. Add to the cooled carrot mixture and stir just enough to remove all the lumps of flour.

Spread into an oil-sprayed 9 x 13-inch pan (or two 9 x 9-inch pans) and bake 45 minutes to 1 hour, until a toothpick inserted into the center comes out clean.

When the cake is completely cooled, frost it with White Delight Frosting or Tofu Cream Frosting (see page 148).

Per serving: 315 calories; 5 g protein; 58 g carbohydrate; 7 g fat; 200 mg sodium; 0 mg cholesterol

Magic Chocolate Cake

Makes one 9-inch cake

What's magic about this cake? It contains no eggs, no dairy, and it's super-easy to make: it's mixed right in the baking dish!

1 1/2	**cups unbleached flour**
3/4	**cup sugar or other sweetener**
1/2	**teaspoon salt**
1	**teaspoon baking soda**
3	**tablespoons cocoa powder**
1	**teaspoon vanilla**
1/3	**cup vegetable oil**
1	**tablespoon vinegar**
1	**cup cold water**

Preheat the oven to 350°F. Combine the flour, sugar, salt, baking soda, and cocoa powder in a 9 x 9-inch baking dish and stir with a fork until mixed. Make a well in the center and add the vanilla, oil, vinegar, and water. Stir with a fork until well mixed. Clean the sides of the dish with a rubber spatula. Bake in the preheated oven for 30 minutes, until a toothpick inserted in center comes out clean.

Cool completely, then frost with Chocolate Cream Frosting (below).

Chocolate Cream Frosting

Makes enough for one 9-inch cake

2	**tablespoon Spectrum Naturals Spread or softened margarine**
1 1/3	**cups powdered sugar**
1/3	**cup cocoa**
1/2	**teaspoon vanilla**
2-4	**tablespoons water**

Cream the Spectrum Spread or margarine in a small bowl then add the sugar, cocoa, vanilla, and enough water to make a thick but spreadable frosting.

Per serving: 293 calories; 3 g protein; 49 g carbohydrate; 9 g fat; 234 mg sodium; 0 mg cholesterol

Banana Cake

Serves 9

This moist, flavorful cake really doesn't need frosting. The walnuts are optional, though they do add a lot of flavor and texture.

2	**cups unbleached or whole wheat pastry flour**
1 1/2	**teaspoons baking soda**
1/2	**teaspoon salt**
1	**cup sugar or other sweetener**
1/3	**cup oil**
4	**ripe bananas, mashed (about 2 1/2 cups)**
1/4	**cup water**
1	**teaspoon vanilla**
1	**cup chopped walnuts (optional)**

Preheat the oven to 350°F. Mix the flour, baking soda, and salt together.

In a large bowl, beat the sugar and oil together, then add the bananas and mash them. Stir in the water and vanilla and mix thoroughly. Add the flour mixture, along with the chopped walnuts, and stir to mix. Spread into an oil-sprayed 9 x 9-inch pan, and bake at 350°F for 45 to 50 minutes, until a toothpick inserted into the center comes out clean.

Per serving (with nuts): 330 calories; 5 g protein; 50 g carbohydrate; 11 g fat; 256 mg sodium; 0 mg cholesterol

Per serving (without nuts): 280 calories; 3 g protein; 50 g carbohydrate; 7 g fat; 256 mg sodium; 0 mg cholesterol

Applesauce Cake

Serves 9

2	**cups unbleached or whole wheat pastry flour**
1/2	**teaspoon salt**
1 1/2	**teaspoons baking soda**
1 1/2	**teaspoons cinnamon**
1/4	**teaspoon ginger**
1/8	**teaspoon cloves**
1/3	**cup oil**
3/4	**cup sugar or other sweetener**
1 1/2	**cups unsweetened applesauce**
1/2	**cup raisins**
1/2	**cup chopped walnuts (optional)**

Preheat the oven to 350°F. Combine the flour, salt, baking soda, cinnamon, ginger, and cloves.

In a separate bowl, beat the oil and sugar together, then stir in the applesauce and mix thoroughly. Add the flour mixture gradually to the applesauce mixture. Beat until smooth, then stir in the raisins and walnuts. Pour into an oil-sprayed 9 x 9-inch pan and bake for 45 to 50 minutes. Serve plain or frosted with White Delight Frosting (page 148).

Per serving: 254 calories; 3 g protein; 44 g carbohydrate; 7 g fat; 257 mg sodium; 0 mg cholesterol

White Delight Frosting

Makes about 1 cup

2	cups powdered sugar
1/4	cup Spectrum Naturals Spread or softened margarine
1	teaspoon vanilla
1-2	tablespoons soy milk or rice milk

Combine the powdered sugar, Spectrum Spread or margarine, and vanilla in a bowl and beat with an electric mixer until smooth, adding just enough soy milk or rice milk to make the frosting spreadable. Makes enough for one 9 x 9-inch cake.

Per tablespoon: 57 calories; 0 g protein; 12 g carbohydrate; 1 g fat; 26 mg sodium; 0 mg cholesterol

Tofu Cream Frosting

Makes about 1 cup

1/2	pound very firm tofu
1	tablespoon canola oil
1	tablespoon lemon juice
1/3	cup brown rice syrup or corn syrup
1/2	teaspoon vanilla

Combine all of the ingredients in a blender or food processor and blend until completely smooth. Makes enough for one 9 x 9-inch cake.

Per tablespoon: 43 calories; 2 g protein; 7 g carbohydrate; 1 g fat; 45 mg sodium; 0 mg cholesterol

Pumpkin Custard Pie

Makes one 9 or 10-inch pie

Cornstarch replaces eggs as the thickener in this traditional pie. Use a commercially prepared crust, or any of the crusts on pages 151 or 152.

1	**9 or 10-inch pie crust**
1/2	**cup sugar or other sweetener**
4	**tablespoons cornstarch**
1	**teaspoon cinnamon**
1/2	**teaspoon ginger**
1/8	**teaspoon cloves**
1/2	**teaspoon salt**
1	**15-ounce can solid-pack pumpkin**
1 1/2	**cups soy milk or rice milk**

Preheat the oven to 350°F. In a large bowl, stir together the sugar, cornstarch, spices, and salt. Blend in the pumpkin and soy milk or rice milk, then pour into a 9 or 10-inch crust and bake until set, about 45 minutes. Cool before cutting.

Per serving: 150 calories; 3 g protein; 33 g carbohydrate; 0 g fat; 252 mg sodium; 0 mg cholesterol

Sweet Surprise Pumpkin Pie

Makes one 9 or 10-inch pie

No one will guess that the thickener in this pie is agar, a seaweed available in natural food stores. Use a commercially prepared crust or one of the crusts on pages 151 or 152.

1	**9 or 10-inch pie crust**
1 1/2	**cups soy milk or rice milk**
3	**tablespoons agar flakes**
1	**15-ounce can solid-pack pumpkin**
1/2	**cup sugar or other sweetener**
1	**teaspoon cinnamon**
1/2	**teaspoon ginger**
1/8	**teaspoon cloves**
1/2	**teaspoon salt**

Preheat the oven to 350°F. Combine the soy milk or rice milk and agar in a saucepan and let stand 5 minutes. Bring to a simmer over medium heat and cook 2 minutes, stirring constantly. Stir in the remaining ingredients and blend well. Pour into a 9 or 10-inch crust and bake for 45 minutes. Cool before cutting.

Per serving: 134 calories; 3 g protein; 30 g carbohydrate; 0 g fat; 252 mg sodium; 0 mg cholesterol

Tofu Cheesecake

Makes one cheesecake

This smooth and velvety "cheesecake," is delicious topped with fresh fruit and the simple lemon glaze below. Agar flakes, which are made from seaweed, are used as a thickener. Look for them in natural food stores or Asian markets.

1	9-inch baked crumb crust
2	tablespoons agar flakes
2/3	cup soy milk or rice milk
1/2	cup sugar or other sweetener
1/2	teaspoon salt
1	pound reduced-fat firm tofu
4	tablespoons lemon juice
2	teaspoons grated lemon peel
2	teaspoons vanilla

Combine the agar and soy milk or rice milk in a saucepan and let stand 5 minutes. Stir in the sugar and salt. Simmer over low heat, stirring frequently, for 5 minutes.

Pour into a blender and add the tofu, lemon juice, lemon peel, and vanilla. Blend until very smooth. Spread evenly into a pre-baked crust. Top with the Lemon Glaze which follows, and fresh fruit if desired.

Lemon Glaze:

1/3	cup sugar or other sweetener
1 1/2	tablespoons cornstarch or arrowroot powder
1 1/2	tablespoons lemon juice
1/2	teaspoon grated lemon peel
1/3	cup water

fresh fruit for topping (strawberries, kiwi fruit, mandarin oranges, etc.)

Stir the sugar and cornstarch together in a small saucepan then add the lemon juice, lemon peel, and water. Whisk smooth. Heat, stirring constantly, until the mixture is clear and thick. Spread evenly over the cheesecake. Top with fresh fruit. Chill thoroughly before serving.

Per serving: 192 calories; 8 g protein; 36 g carbohydrate; 2 g fat; 247 mg sodium; 0 mg cholesterol

Whole Wheat Pastry Crust

Makes two single crusts or one double crust

2	cups whole wheat pastry flour
1/2	teaspoon salt
1/2	cup cold margarine or vegetable shortening
6-8	tablespoons ice water

Mix the flour and salt, then cut in the margarine until the mixture resembles coarse cornmeal. Add the water, mixing just enough to make a smooth ball of dough. Divide the dough in half and roll each half out on a floured board. Transfer to a 9 or 10-inch pie pan.

For a prebaked crust, prick in several places with a fork, and bake in a preheated 425°F oven until golden brown, about 12 minutes. Otherwise, fill and bake as directed.

Per serving: 85 calories; 2 g protein; 10 g carbohydrate; 4 g fat; 117 mg sodium; 0 mg cholesterol

Fat-free Pie Crust

Makes one 9-inch crust

This crust is slightly sweet and chewy. I use it regularly as a substitute for crumb crusts, and often find it appropriate in place of a regular pastry crust. In addition to being fat-free, it is blessedly easy to prepare.

1	cup Grape-Nuts cereal
1/4	cup apple juice concentrate (undiluted)

Preheat oven to 350°F. Mix the Grape-Nuts and apple juice concentrate and pat into a 9-inch pie pan. Bake for 8 minutes. Cool before filling.

Per serving: 68 calories; 2 g protein; 15 g carbohydrate; 0 g fat; 97 mg sodium; 0 mg cholesterol

Tender Almond Pie Crust

Makes one 10-inch crust

The next best thing to a fat-free pie crust is a crust made with no refined fats or oils. This easy crust is made with almonds, which add wonderful flavor to any pie.

2/3	**cup almonds**
2/3	**cup whole wheat pastry flour**
1	**tablespoon sugar**
1/4	**teaspoon salt**
2	**tablespoons water**

Toast the almonds in a 350°F oven for 15 minutes. Cool completely. Grind into fine pieces in a food processor, then mix in the flour, sugar, and salt. Add the water and mix thoroughly. The dough should be just moist enough to hold together. Press into a 10-inch pie pan. Bake at 350°F for 12 minutes. Cool before filling.

Per serving: 90 calories; 3 g protein; 9 g carbohydrate; 5 g fat; 55 mg sodium; 0 mg cholesterol

Graham Cracker Crust

Makes one 9 or 10-inch crust

2	**cups crushed graham crackers**
1/4	**cup Spectrum Spread or margarine**
2	**tablespoons sugar or other sweetener**

Preheat the oven to 350°F. Combine the finely crushed graham crackers with the Spectrum Spread or margarine and sugar. Mix thoroughly. Press into a 9 or 10-inch pie pan and bake until the edges are lightly browned, about 10 minutes. Cool before filling.

Per serving: 88 calories; 1 g protein; 9 g carbohydrate; 5 g fat; 112 mg sodium; 0 mg cholesterol

Strawberry Smoothie

Serves 2

The secret to making a great smoothie is using frozen fruit which makes it really thick and cold. Frozen strawberries are available in most markets, or you can freeze your own. To freeze the bananas, peel and break them into inch-long pieces. Place loosely in an airtight container to freeze. Bananas will keep in the freezer for about a month, strawberries for six months.

Although the recipe indicates specific measurements, the amounts are really quite flexible. Use roughly equal amounts of strawberries and bananas and add just enough apple juice to enable the blender to operate.

1	**large frozen banana, cut into 1-inch pieces**
1	**cup frozen strawberries**
1/2-1	**cup unsweetened apple juice**

Place the banana chunks and strawberries into the blender with about 1/2 cup of apple juice. Hold the lid on tightly and blend on high speed until thick and smooth. Stop the blender occasionally and move the unblended fruit to the center with a spatula. Add a bit more juice if needed to completely blend the fruit. Serve immediately.

Per serving: 116 calories; 1 g protein; 27 g carbohydrate; 0 g fat; 8 mg sodium; 0 mg cholesterol

Banana Date Freeze

Serves 2

Frozen bananas, soy milk or rice milk, and pitted dates make a thick, rich-tasting frozen dessert. Freeze the peeled bananas in inch-long pieces in an airtight container.

1/2	**cup soy milk or rice milk**
4-6	**pitted dates**
2	**cups frozen banana chunks**

Place the soy milk or rice milk and dates in a blender and process on high speed for 1 minute. Add the frozen bananas and process until thick and smooth, stopping the blender occasionally to stir any unblended chunks to the center.

Per serving: 143 calories; 3 g protein; 30 g carbohydrate; 1 g fat; 46 mg sodium; 0 mg cholesterol

Cranberry Apple Punch

Makes 6 cups

This beverage is the perfect mix of sweet, tart, and spicy flavors. It is made with Cranberry Cove Tea, a Celestial Seasonings product available in many grocery stores and in natural food stores. The punch is delicious cold or hot.

4 1/2	**cups water**
8	**Cranberry Cove Tea bags**
1	**12-ounce can apple juice concentrate**

Bring the water to a boil, then turn off the heat and add the tea bags. Steep at least fifteen minutes. Remove the tea bags and add the apple juice concentrate. Stir to mix.

For a hot beverage, heat in a crockpot or large pot until steamy. Add a few orange and lemon slices as a garnish before serving.

For a cold beverage, chill thoroughly, then serve over ice.

Per serving: 89 calories; 0 g protein; 22 g carbohydrate; 0 g fat; 14 mg sodium; 0 mg cholesterol

Index

About the Author

Jennifer Raymond is a popular cooking and nutrition instructor throughout the United States. She works as a chef and nutrition specialist with Dean Ornish, M.D. in his "Open Your heart" program, teaching patients how a delicious, easily-prepared vegetarian diet can reverse heart disease. She has served as a nutrition consultant and guest chef for the employee fitness programs of several major corporations and health spas. In addition, she has worked with the federal government's Nutrition Education Training Project to improve the nutritional quality of the national school lunch program. Her first cookbook, _The Best of Jenny's Kitchen_, was published by Avon Books in 1981 and was followed closely by her television series _Cooking—Naturally!_ Jennifer lives in Calistoga, California with her husband Stephen Avis and their five dogs.